Leica Q3 43 User Guidebook

A Comprehensive Step-by-Step Manual for Utilizing the Leica Q3 43 Camera from Beginners to Experts

Torren Mercy

CHAPTER ONE
REVIEW OF THE LEICA Q3 43

A variation of Leica's full-frame prime lens compact, the Q3 43 features a 43mm F2 lens positioned in front of a 60MP BSI CMOS sensor. Other than that, it is identical to the original 28mm Q3. What distinguishes the two is the longer lens, the grey leatherette covering, and the number inscribed on the hotshoe.

Important details

- 43mm F2 image stabilized lens
- 60MP BSI CMOS full-frame sensor
- Options to crop in to 60, 75, 90, 120 or 150mm equiv focal lengths
- 5.76M dot OLED EVF with 0.79x magnification
- 3" tilt touchscreen LCD with 1.8 million dots
- Native ISO range of 100-100,000 (ISO 50 manually selectable)
- Hybrid autofocus (PDAF + contrast AF with DFD)
- Continuous shooting up to 15fps (7fps with AF-C)
- 8K video capture in UHD or DCI ratios up to 30p (H.265)
- Apple ProRes 422HQ support for 1080p video capture up to 60p
- AI-assisted perspective control and dynamic range tools for JPEG mode
- IP52-rated dust and water resistant
- Wi-Fi and Bluetooth with connection to Leica Fotos app
- Wireless charging via optional hand grip add-on

The Leica Q3 43 will go on sale today for a suggested price of $6895, which is about $900 (15%) more than the Q3 was when it was first released, despite the fact that the price has since increased by $300. It will cost $250 for an optional auxiliary grip that adds Arca-compatible flanges for tripod attachment and a more noticeable hand-hold.

Advantages

- Excellent JPEG and Raw picture quality
- Even at the widest aperture setting, the lens performs admirably.
- Autofocus is quick and accurate.
- Flash synchronization throughout the entire (mechanical) shutter speed range
- At high ISOs, very light luminance noise reduction helps maintain detail.
- The tool for perspective correction is really useful.
- Additional versatility is provided by digital zoom options.
- Excellent codec and bitrate selection in a very detailed video
- Good battery life
- You'll be able to identify your Leica.

Disadvantages

- AF point selection is incompatible with subject recognition.
- Subject recognition is less reliable than with other of the cameras we examined.
- Auto white balance has the ability to be cool or aggressively neutral.
- In low light, photos with minimal default luma noise reduction are extremely noisy.
- The switch from AF to MF button is difficult.
- Accessing the auto ISO settings is difficult.
- It's important to understand how digital zoom affects image quality.
- Notable rolling shutter in its most intricate video settings
- Strong video specifications, but no audio out
- Above 30p, a 4K capture exhibits significant aliasing.
- Significantly higher cost for the Leica brand

If you are not satisfied with the angle of view provided by the current 28mm Q cameras, the Leica Q3 43 is a welcome addition to the lineup and a stunning example of engineering and design. With a lens that is extremely sharp and has good cross-frame consistency even at wide apertures, the image quality is excellent. Additionally, the controls on the camera are pleasantly centered on the basics of photography, which is a welcome change from the feature and symbol overload that much of the industry has become accustomed to.

To ensure that the screw-in hood lines up precisely when it is fully tightened, the thread on the front of the lens has been clipped. It seems to be a reflection of the camera's meticulous attention to detail. There were a few peculiarities about the camera that seemed appropriate for its potential usage. The autofocus UI feels a generation or two behind the competition, despite the fact that autofocus was quick and responsive. It might be nearly impossible to maintain the camera's focus on your favorite subject when shooting candids because of its face detection mode, which ignores your selected AF point. Additionally, the Auto white balance mode on the Q3 43 can be extremely literal, eliminating any color cast in the scene and appearing to err on the side of a pretty cool depiction. This is a little off-putting, but not an issue if you're shooting Raw. The majority of contemporary cameras understand that sometimes you want to maintain part of the scene's atmosphere, or at the very least, keep the colors on the more pleasing side of neutral. It also takes some getting used to the very passive approach to luminance noise.

Leica Q3 43: What Is New?

Regarding what's new, the response is a contradictory compromise between "very little" and "everything." The lens's focal length and, by extension, the crop modes' corresponding focal lengths are the only significant feature changes in the Q3 43. It's a brand-new design with eight groups of eleven lenses, including seven aspheric [per a design patented by Panasonic]. It has Leica's 'APO' logo, which denotes an apochromatic design that should reduce longitudinal chromatic aberration and maximize sharpness. For people who are more accustomed to 28mm, 35mm, or 50mm focal lengths, the 43mm focal length may seem odd, but there is a reason for using it. Since the diagonal length of a full-frame sensor is 43mm, a 43mm lens is neither somewhat telephoto like a 50mm nor slightly wide-angle like a 35mm.

As a result, the camera is more versatile than a fixed 50mm and more different from the current 28mm Q3 than a 35mm. I quickly got used to the 43's ideal normal vision of the world, but as someone who regularly uses the 35mm focal length, I found myself missing the slightly wider view I had grown accustomed to. Anyone who has ever used a 28mm lens on APS-C, Nikon's 40mm F2 on Z-mount, Pentax's 43mm F1.9 Limited, or Panasonic's 20mm F1.7 on Micro Four Thirds will feel right at home. It intuitively feels like it catches "the world in front of me," but I won't claim that it matches the human field of view because humans don't see a single field of view simultaneously and with the same acuity throughout the picture (our eyes don't function like cameras). To determine if the Q3 or Q3 43 is best for you, you don't really need to use the camera; all you need to do is decide if you want to be able to be a little more selective or if you prefer to take a broad shot that includes a lot of the scene. That's how easy it is.

About 'Macro' capabilities

Note: When you rotate the ring closest to the camera (on the right side of this picture), a new distance scale that displays the lens's close focus range slides forward from the barrel.

The 43mm lens has been developed with a close-up option, just as the earlier Q cameras. Selecting the 'Macro' position on the ring closest to the camera activates this. In the process, a closer focus range is indicated by a distance scale that pushes forward in place of the regular scale. The distance scale's default setting shows a range of 0.6m (23.6") to infinity. This minimum focus distance is reduced to 0.27m (10.6") when switching to the Macro position and it now reaches its maximum of 0.6m.

The Crop modes and triple resolution

With 60, 75, 90, 120, and 150mm equivalent crops of its sensor of roughly 31, 21, 14, 8, and 5MP, respectively, the Q3 maximizes its high-resolution sensor. In addition to lowering the available resolution, cropping in also uses a smaller and smaller area of the sensor, which naturally results in poorer image quality and poorer light performance. The smaller sensor photographs will appear worse when magnified or viewed at a standard size, but the pixel-level IQ will appear the same. Since its well into the realm of tiny cameras at 150mm equiv, it's probably best to use it only in well-lit conditions.

	Crop factor	Pixel Count (MP)	Approx sensor dimensions
43mm	1.0x	60.3	36 x 24mm
60mm equiv.	1.4x	30.8	26 x 17mm
75mm equiv.	1.7x	20.9	21 x 14mm
90mm equiv.	2.1x	13.9	17 x 12mm
120mm equiv	2.8x	7.8	13 x 9mm
150mm equiv.	3.5x	5.0	10.3 x 6.9

If you are not constantly in need of 60MP files, the Q3 43's complete sensor can also produce 36 or 18MP files. Compared to utilizing a 36 or 18MP camera, these should have more detail because they are downsampled from the original shot. You can choose the output size for JPEGs and Raw separately, so if you can think of a good reason, you can choose small JPEGs with full-sized Raws or lower-resolution Raws with full-sized JPEGs.

The Leica Looks

The Q3 43 allows you to download up to six 'Leica Looks' through the Leica Fotos app, in addition to the 'Film Style' color options that are already pre-installed on the camera. The difference is that Leica Looks are presets that cannot be altered, while Film Styles allow you to change parameters like contrast, saturation, and sharpening. There are now seven Leica Looks available thanks to the addition of Leica Chrome in the most recent version of the Fotos app. This can be mounted on the SL3 or either of the Q3 cameras. However, in contrast to the SL3, the quick settings page is not editable, so if you use Leica Looks instead of Film Styles, you cannot add them to that menu.

The Perspective correction

Note: The clever perspective correction option is a good way to get a straightened image out the camera; however it may work better with the wide-angle lens of the original Q3.

Leica's perspective correcting capability is present in the Q3 43. When activated, this scans the scene for convergent lines that it believes should be parallel and uses that information to determine the appropriate corrections. Only the JPEG image receives the changes; the raw, unaltered version can be preserved as well. The JPEG is rescaled to the resolution at which you are using the camera at the moment.

The way it compares

No additional prime-lens compacts with a 43mm (or equivalent) field of view are available. The Ricoh GR IIIx, with its integrated 40mm equivalent prime lens, is the most obvious peer. Its 24MP APS-C sensor makes it smaller and less costly than the Leica, but it cannot match the Leica's image quality and resolution. Before you take into account how the Ricoh's smaller sensor affects depth-of-field and whole-image light collection, the lens is a stop slower in absolute terms. Although we found it far easier to adjust to the 43mm field of vision from 35mm equiv than it is to switch back and forth between 35 and 28mm, Fujifilm's X100 VI has a wider, 35mm equiv lens. The cameras themselves are also somewhat different. The Leica is full-frame and employs a traditional EVF, while the Fujifilm has an intriguing optical/electronic hybrid viewfinder and an APS-C sensor.

	Leica Q3 43	Leica Q3	Ricoh GR IIIx	Fujifilm X100VI
MSRP (body)	$6895	$5995	$999	$1599
Sensor	60 MP full-frame (Bayer)	60MP full-frame (Bayer)	24MP APS-C (Bayer)	40MP APS-C (X-Trans)
Lens	43mm F2.0	28mm F1.7	40mm equiv. F2.8	35mm equiv. F2.0
Built-in ND filter	No (accepts 49mm filters)	No (accepts 49mm filters)	2.0 EV	4.0 EV
ISO range	50-100,000	50-100,000	100-102400	100-51200
Viewfinder type	5.76M dot OLED electronic	5.76M dot OLED electronic	Optical (optional)	3.69M-dot OLED electronic / optical hybrid
LCD	3" tilting 1.84M dots	3" tilting 1.84M dots	3" fixed 1.037M dots	3" tilting 1.62M dots

Touch-screen	Yes	Yes	Yes	Yes
Included flash	No	No	No	Built-in
Weather-sealing	Yes (IP52)	Yes (IP52)	No	Yes*
Max. burst	15 fps (12-bit AF-S) 7fps (14-bit AF-C)	15 fps (12-bit AF-S) 7fps (14-bit AF-C)	4 fps	13 fps (elec. shutter) 6 fps (mech shutter)
Max. shutter, mech / electronic	1/2000 / 1/16000	1/2000 / 1/16000	1/4000	1/4000 / 1/180,000
Video	8K/30p, 4K/60p, 1080/120p	8K/30p, 4K/60p, 1080/120p	1080/60p	6.2K/30p, 4K/60p 1080/120p
Battery life (CIPA)	350 shots	350 shots	200 shots	310 shots (EVF)
Weight	772 g	743 g	262 g	521g

Because of its 35mm F2 lens and comparable sized sensor, Sony's long-out-of-production RX1 series would also make a useful comparison, but regrettably, it seems to have been discontinued. All four are based on in-lens 'leaf' shutters, like the majority of fixed-lens cameras. These can sync with flashes across the whole range of their mechanical shutter speed ranges, but they are unable to achieve the 1/8000 sec exposures that high-end focal-plane curtain shutters frequently offer.

The body and the handling

The body of the Q3 43 is nearly the same as that of the Q3, which was a mild redesign of the Q2's design. The main distinction is that the 43 model has the numerals 43 milled into its hotshoe and on its lens, and it has a grey leatherette finish. Without exactly copying Leica's flagship M rangefinder series, the design draws styling inspiration from the company's past, especially from the rounded edges of the body. Even if you hide the red dot mark on the front, the general design and typographic usage are distinctly Leica, even though there is little chance that it will be confused for an M. The controls are rather simple, consisting of an aperture ring and shutter speed dial with 'A' locations to transfer control to the camera. In addition, a command dial with a configurable button in the middle is located on the back shoulder. It is a strategy that assists you in concentrating all of your attention on the basic photographic settings.

Based on your exposure mode, the command dial's Auto setting assumes a distinct function.

Shutter speed dial	Aperture ring setting	Exposure mode	Command dial function (Auto)
A	F-no	Aperture priority	Exposure Comp.
Time value	A	Shutter priority	1/3EV shutter adj
A	A	Flexible Program	F-no
Time value	F-no	Manual Exposure	1/3EV shutter adj

The center button of the four-way controller, which is mostly used for accessing the menus and positioning the AF point, can be customized, and there are two additional custom buttons along the top rear edge of the camera. You can customize any of these buttons by holding them down. By limiting the number of parameters that may be set to each button, you can quickly access the options you want to choose from if you wish to change the buttons' function on a frequent basis. On the lens's lower right corner is a focus tab with a little button. It is necessary to press this button in order to shift the focus ring from the 'Auto' position to manual focus.

The interface

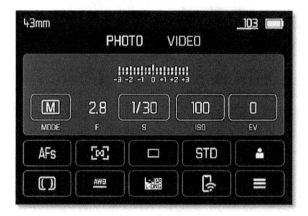

The most recent iteration of the interface that Leica has been developing over the last few years is the Q3 43. A quick settings screen with the exposure settings at the top and a variety of other camera options below is displayed when the menu button is pressed, same like on the Q3 and SL3. The touch-sensitive display allows you to enter video mode by swiping left, which also displays a quick options menu for video settings.

You can navigate through the menu tabs by selecting the Menu button again, which also takes you to Page 1 of the menu itself. Similar to the D-Lux8, this creates the strange possibility that you could press left to go one page to the left, but you would have to press Menu to go the other way (with the four-way joystick, pushing right changes the current setting or opens a sub-menu). Given that there aren't many reasons to visit the main menu, it's a minor oddity that doesn't take long to get used to. Since the Q3 43's interface is similar to that of the original Q3, it does not yet include the SL3's enhancements, such the ability to personalize the quick settings menu or the red color coding for stills and yellow for videos. As an alternative, you can store your preferred menu selections in the 'Favorites' tab, which shows up as the main menus' first page.

The viewfinder

The Q3 43 features the same 1.8M dot (560 x 640px) tiltable touchscreen and 5.76M dot (1600 x 1200px) viewfinder as the current Q3 model. A USB-C plug and a Micro HDMI port are located behind a tiny rubber door on the side of the camera. Although video footage can be broadcast via the HDMI connector, the exact codec and resolution used will depend on whether you're simultaneously recording internally or shooting L-Log, HLG, or regular DR footage. Since the USB port has a 3.1 Gen 2 interface, data transfers of up to 10Gb/s are possible. If you have an iPhone, you can use this to tether to the Leica Fotos app.

The battery

The Q3 43 is powered by the same 16Wh BP-SCL6 battery as the wide-angle Q3. According to the CIPA methodology, the battery life is rated at 350 shots per charge; nevertheless, we frequently find that this number is doubled. For a camera that you will probably want to use for a few days of shooting, 350 is a pretty good rating. Even when the camera is in use, it can be charged via its USB-C port. Additionally, wireless charging is a possibility. The camera may be charged with common Qi wireless chargers if you add an optional handgrip.

Quality of image

A range of textures, colors, and detail kinds that you'll find in the actual world are all simulated in our test scenario. In order to observe the impact of various lighting conditions, it also features two illumination settings. It's a little challenging to know what to compare the Leica Q3 43 to because it has so few direct contemporaries and we haven't always been able to obtain production-spec Leicas long enough to film our test scene. As a result, we will mainly examine its appearance in comparison to the Sony a7R V, which it shares a sensor with. For a fixed-lens camera, the detail levels are excellent, though slightly lower than with the Sony 85mm F1.4 GM lens, particularly in the far corners. Even though Sony seems to be using some kind of processing or noise reduction, the noise levels seem to be lower, if anything. Despite what seems to be very intense sharpening, the Leica's JPEG processor isn't extracting as much detail as the Sony, which results in a slight overshoot at high contrast edges. Very magenta pinks and relatively dark yellows are features of Leica's Standard color response, which is likewise highly rare. Because of its extreme neutrality, the light pink patch usually produces accurate rather than appealing Caucasian skin tones. The chroma noise was aggressively suppressed by the default noise reduction, but the luminance noise levels remained abnormally high. This method preserves detail and creates the appearance of detail, but it also results in extremely high noise levels in the photos. It takes some getting accustomed to, however there is a claim that this luminance speckling is comparable to film grain.

The white balance

Additionally, we discovered that the Q3 43's auto white balance could be off by a neutral or even cold amount. In theory, auto white balance should attempt to eliminate any tint in the lighting, but in reality, most people prefer it to add a little of warmth to the environment. I stopped using Auto white balance because of the following photo, which was taken with daylight coming in through windows behind the camera. JPEGs were looking quite clinical.

The lens performance

Although our test scene isn't intended to be a lens test, it works well for this focal length because it was taken from a respectable distance. Even at its widest F2.0 setting, the lens is incredibly crisp. Only in comparison to stopped-down shots are there a slight loss of corner sharpness and a faint suggestion of vignetting. It's reasonable to say that the lens is superb given that we're examining a 60MP image at the pixel level. Capture one was used to handle these photos, allowing us to use the distortion correction profile provided by the manufacturer while disabling vignetting and lateral chromatic aberration correction. The lens of the Q3 43 is made with mathematically corrected geometric distortion, allowing for optical correction of other aberrations without the need to enlarge and complicate the lens or exacerbate existing aberrations through distortion correction efforts.

Using its 'Summicron' branding, Leica claims that the Q3 43's lens is virtually chromatic aberration-free in both our test scene and real-world photography. Since we are solely concerned with the quality of the final image, we see no point in evaluating a lens's performance once part of its components have been removed. Furthermore, if the corners appear this good after correction, we don't think it matters if glass or mathematics was used to achieve it, especially if it makes the lens this relatively small.

About Autofocus

Like Leica's M-mount lenses, the Q3 43's lens has a tiny focus tab. The focus ring must be released from the autofocus setting into the manual focus range by pressing a little release button on the upper lip. The Q3 43 includes a number of AF settings, including a big zone, multi-field, a shiftable and scaleable AF field, and a basic AF spot. A subject in the scene is chosen using the Eye/Face/Body detection and Eye/Face/Body + Animal detection modes. After that, you can choose from a list of recognized subjects by pressing the four-way controller. The Q3

43's autofocus is incredibly silent and surprisingly quick. Because we don't think it accurately captures the kinds of autofocus challenges that a camera with a 43mm lens may encounter, we didn't put it through our regular autofocus test. The camera was very fast for a fixed prime compact throughout the great majority of our use, with the exception of one hurried photo in which it claimed to be in focus but wasn't. One problem we did run into, though, was that the Q3 43's detection modes do not let you to pre-select a subject by specifying an AF point. This is disheartening, and we discovered that while attempting to take candid pictures with several individuals, we had to disable face identification because the camera would continuously switch between subjects and identify and lose faces more quickly than we could choose them. We haven't come across a subject recognition system that doesn't function with a chosen AF point in a long time, and we discovered that it made autofocus operation more difficult and slower, at least in some situations. However, this was the only significant complaint we had about the AF. In general, it's quick and self-assured enough that you don't need to worry about it too much.

Video

With features including up to 8K/30 capture and ProRes 422HQ footage at up to 1080/60, the Q3 43 has some very ambitious video specs. Up to 29 minutes of video can be captured using the camera. According to Leica, options for connecting external microphones via the USB port will be available starting in October.

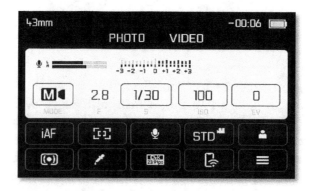

The video settings menu is displayed when you slide left on the screen after pressing the menu button to access video capture. After that, a variety of codecs and resolutions are available for selection.

	File type	Frame rates	Codec	Bit-depth / Chroma	Bitrate
DCI 8K	MOV	29.97, 25, 24, 23.98	H.265	10-bit 4:2:0	300Mbps
UHD 8K	MP4				
DCI 4K	MOV	59.94, 50, 48, 47.95	H.264	10-bit 4:2:2	600Mbps
		29.97, 25, 24, 23.98			400Mbps
UHD 4K		59.94, 50, 48, 47.95			600Mbps
		29.97, 25, 24, 23.98			400Mbps
	MP4	59.94, 50	H.265	10-bit 4:2:0	100Mbps
		29.97, 25, 23.98	H.264	8-bit 4:2:0	100Mbps

In 8K, a great deal of detail is captured. In both 8K and 4K modes, UHD footage is virtually identical to DCI footage, with the edges cut off. Using the same sensor readout as the 8K modes, 4K footage up to 30p displays detail levels similar to those of the oversampled 'HQ' modes on the Canon EOS R5 II. Frame rates higher than 30p are sub-sampled; 50% line skipping is suggested by the halved rolling shutter rate. These modes have noticeable moiré in addition to being less detailed. Regretfully, rolling shutter rates are rather large even though detail capture is high. The majority of modes have a rolling shutter of more than 30 ms, which makes them highly susceptible to twisted and warped motion if you pan or move objects across the camera quickly.

	Rolling shutter rate
8K or 4K footage up to 29.97p	31.3ms (1/32 sec)
4K footage at 47.95p upwards	15.5ms (1/64 sec)

As the movement to correct shake can both counteract and worsen the distortion caused by the delayed reading, rolling shutter can also interact awkwardly with stabilizing attempts, resulting in the so-called 'Jello' effect. Given how great the specs appear on paper, the results are a touch disappointing, but we don't consider video to be a particularly important feature on a camera with a fixed 43mm lens and no way to check audio.

For whom is this camera intended?

The Leica Q3 43 is designed for a niche market of those who appreciate photography as an art form and are willing to shell out a lot of cash for a very specific yet high-quality tool. This camera is ideal for photographers who want simple settings and capabilities found in more mainstream cameras to high-quality photographs, craftsmanship, and ease of use. For those who prefer a full-frame sensor in a compact design without the hassle of interchangeable lenses, it's fantastic. First off, if you want straightforward photography and don't want to carry around a large DSLR or a number of lenses, the Leica Q3 43 can be a decent option. The fixed 43mm f/2 lens on this camera offers a "normal" field of view. Because of this, it's excellent for portraits, street photography, and even some landscape photography. For those who would rather not bother about the technicalities and instead concentrate on composition and capturing the moment, this is also excellent. The Q3 43 will be a huge hit with photographers who appreciate how meticulously Leica designs its cameras. The company has a long history of producing cameras that are user-friendly and seem natural. It's the same with this model. It is intended for those who enjoy taking photos by hand but yet wish to utilize modern photo technology, such as high-resolution cameras and auto focus. Additionally, fans and semi-professionals looking for a high-end camera that blends in with the background are likely to find this camera appealing. Compared to other cameras in its class, it is significantly less conspicuous, which makes it ideal for street photojournalists who wish to capture unplanned events without attracting too much attention. But given its expensive cost, it's probably not for novices or casual photographers who don't give a damn about Leica's past or who seek the highest image quality in a compact package. Despite having some contemporary features, the Q3 43 is likely only worth the premium price for people who understand Leica's design philosophy and value sharpness, outstanding image quality, and the distinctive appearance of the brand. For photographers who are true art lovers who are willing to spend money on a camera that offers them excellent image quality, accuracy, and a customized photographic experience, there is the Leica Q3 43. If you appreciate taking pictures and want it to feel more like an extension of who you are, this might be the perfect camera for you.

Comprehending the Leica Philosophy

Leica's philosophy is founded on accuracy, simplicity, and a nearly sacred perspective on photography. You will immediately realize that a Leica feels different from other cameras when you hold one in your hands. Creating an experience that allows you to connect with your subject is more important than just the technical details or specifications. Leica has long been recognized for producing cameras with little features that are superfluous. Rather, they emphasize the shooting technique itself. The commitment to excellence that underpins Leica's design is evident in both the camera body and the accompanying lenses. Many photojournalists find it challenging to duplicate their lenses' renowned clarity, vivid color reproduction, and unique "look" with other gear. Leica lenses are frequently commended for their unparalleled optical performance, live image ring photographs with exceptional clarity, and soft and beautiful bokeh, particularly the 43mm f/2 APO-Summicron on the Q3 43. Despite using digital technology, Leica emphasizes the need of manual size control in its cameras. Only the most crucial components are frequently included in the construction of their cameras. It won't be too difficult to navigate a Leica's buttons and menus. Giving the shooter a sense of control and encouraging them to concentrate on framing, exposure, and composition rather than all the settings is the main goal instead. A more organic and creative process results from each dial and button feeling like an extension of the photographer's body.

A key concept in Leica's philosophy is "camera as an instrument." A camera should inspire your creativity and be more than just a tool for taking photos. It's a popular misperception that picture graphs from Leica cameras are more than just simple recordings. With a feel and functionality that allows you to interact with your environment and the subjects you're taking, the company's design philosophy aims to create cameras that become unique to their owners. Leica is a firm believer in creating durable products. Both in terms of quality and design, these cameras are renowned for their extended lifespan. Leica cameras tend to have a timeless appearance and are built to last, both in terms of longevity and the value they provide to their owners. A Leica camera, in contrast to many other contemporary gadgets, is built to last for many years. As you improve as a shooter and a person, you can use it. Leica wants the realm of photography to unite people. Photographers who appreciate the brand's attitude, design, and image quality have become its loyal supporters. Because Leica cameras have a sense of exclusivity, people who own and use them frequently feel proud of them. It's not usually because of the cost; rather, it's because Leica embodies a perspective on photography that appeals to those who are interested in more than simply the technical aspects of it. Serious shooters can identify with this mindset, which emphasizes honoring the craft and aiming for image perfection. Making experiences is as much a part of Leica's philosophy as producing cameras. It's about enabling shooters to capture crisp, accurate images of the world as they see it, free from technological interference. The Leica Q3 43, with its straightforward design, excellent optical performance, and user-friendly settings, is the ideal embodiment of this notion. Photographers who wish to immerse themselves in the art of creating images and experience photography in its most unadulterated state should use this camera.

The Leica Q Series: From the Leica Q to the Q3 43

In 2015, Leica introduced the Q line of digital full-frame cameras, which have a fixed, non-changeable primary lens and a combined frame rate mode. The Q family's success can be attributed to its iconic Leica design, excellent lens quality, craftsmanship, high-quality images, and affordable price when compared to other Leica cameras. The Leica Q (Typ 116), a full-frame fixed-lens camera with a Leica Summilux 28mm lens and an aperture range of f/1.7 to f/16, was the first model to be released in 2015. For 35mm and 50mm lenses, it can digitally zoom up to 1.25x or 1.8x, respectively. Various variations have been produced over time, including the Leica Q Khaki, the Leica Q Silver, and the Leica Q Titanium Grey paint treatment. The technical specifications of these versions are identical to those of the original. A little different was the Leica Q-P, which was released in 2018. However, the red dot logo was absent. Rather, the shutter release button was changed, similar to the Leica M and CL cameras, and the iconic Leica inscription was carved on the top plate.

The Leica Q2 was released in 2019 following the release of the Leica Q-P and the original Leica Q. It was referred to as the Q line's next-generation model in advertising. Along with the same Summilux 28mm f/1.7 prime lens and a brand-new 47.3MP CMOS full-frame sensor, it also included additional features including a digital frame selection for 35, 50, and 75mm and a dust and water-resistant cover for shooting in all weather. Other Leica Q2 design options included the Leica Q2 Reporter, which featured Kevlar trim instead of leather; the Leica Q2 007 Edition, which was named after James Bond's 25th mission, "No Time to Die"; the Leica Q2 "Ghost" by Hodinkee, which featured a chic grey leather trim to honor the iconic diving watch known as the "Ghost Bezel"; the Leica Q2 Disney "100 Years of Wonder" version, which featured a Mickey Mouse print on the plate to commemorate Disney's 100th anniversary; and, lastly, the one I believe is the most exquisite: the limited special edition Leica Q2 "Dawn" by musician Seal, which honors the artist's soulful lyrics and comes with a scarf that matches. In 2020, the Leica Q2 Monochrom was introduced. It is the ideal camera for lovers of black-and-white photography because it is the only full-frame compact camera with a dedicated monochrome sensor. A reporter's version of the camera is also available. In 2023, the Leica Q3—the third generation of the Leica Q family—was released. It features a stabilised Summilux 28mm f/1.7 lens and a 60MP CMOS full-frame sensor. Additionally, it can be digitally cropped to focal lengths of 35, 50, 75, and 90 mm. The Leica Q3, the first model in the Q line with a high-resolution, tiltable 3-inch LCD, and the ability to record 8K video.

In September 2024, the Leica Q3 43 was released. The Leica Q3 43's primary distinction from previous generations is that it lacks the conventional 28mm focal length. Rather, it features a digital zoom that allows you to adjust the focal length to 60, 75, 90, 120, or 150mm, and an APO-Summicron lens with a fixed focal length of 43mm f/2. It is said that the 43mm lens can capture moments as they are perceived by the eye. This is so that the topic can be captured in a natural, balanced, and lifelike manner because the focal length is so close to human eyesight. Like the previous Leica Q models, the Q3 43 and Q3 both have a tiltable touchscreen and a combined macro mode. Leica claims that the new lens is extremely crisp, however I don't know enough about photography to describe the distinction between Summilux and Summicron lenses. Its intricate apochromatically adjusted optical design, which features four aspherical elements, produces pleasing colors in a variety of lighting conditions. These lenses are regarded as some of the best available. The APO lens should also allow you to use short exposure times, even in low light conditions, thanks to its excellent ISO range (from 50 to 100000).

My initial thoughts on Leica Q2 vs. Leica Q3 43

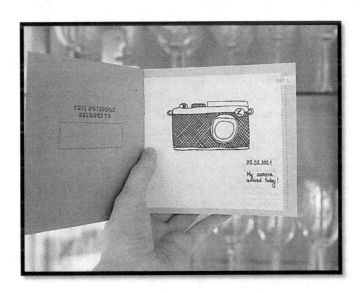

It took me some time to get acclimated to my Leica Q2 after I purchased it in 2021. I had to adjust to a 28mm mode because of my Canon setup. Although I had seen numerous videos of photographers lauding the iconic Leica appearance, I wasn't very thrilled with the initial results. In addition, shortly after I bought it, I had to replace it with another lens since the fabric of the lens cap broke off, rendering it worthless. In my opinion, the original lens cap is quite shoddy, which is not what you would anticipate from a Leica camera, which is renowned for its high-quality, long-lasting lenses. I prefer to employ a lot of bokeh to give my shots a dreamier appearance, thus I don't think the Leica Q2 was the ideal option for me. It's not the camera's fault because I was aware that Leica cameras are known for their more direct and documentary approach to street photography.

After a difficult beginning, I began to enjoy the camera's additional functions. In comparison to my previous Canon setup, the Q2 felt incredibly light, and I like how crisp the photo graphs were. I can assure you that you will see every detail when you enlarge a Leica photo! The issue is that it takes hours to resize the large photo files in Photoshop. Even though I have a decent laptop for editing, resizing a collection of photographs without erasing any information still takes a long time. Additionally, connecting the camera to the Leica app takes some time. But after it does, everything functions as it should. I can't imagine taking images without the Leica Q2, which is now my only camera for travel. Now that I'm accustomed to it, I appreciate the way the pictures appear despite its small size and light weight. It is really important to me that they look very natural. Because it has interchangeable lenses, I still prefer my Canon camera for photos, products, and flowers. I prefer a 35mm lens length for portraiture since it is less distorted. I was ecstatic when Leica revealed the Q3 43 because I believed I had discovered my ideal camera. The "human perspective" section was excellent. The images on the Leica website were stunning, and the increased lens length is excellent for portraiture. In addition, I was eager to see how the bokeh would seem. During a Leica photo walk in Klagenfurt in November, I had the opportunity to test out the Leica Q3 43.

The color of the body (the Q2 is black, while the Q3 43 is gray) and the shutter button were the two most obvious differences between the Leica Q3 43 and the Q2. If you know how to use the Leica Q2, it's easy to learn how to take images with the Q3 43. I never imagined this, but it appears that I have already become accustomed to my Leica Q2's 28mm lens, and it will continue to be my preferred option for street and travel photography. I felt the 43mm was too "zoomed in," so even though I wanted a longer focal length, I had trouble getting good pictures in the city. I was also curious to see how this new Leica lens would affect the bokeh. My Instagram feed mostly consists of pictures of flowers with beautiful bokeh. I couldn't determine whether or not I wanted to keep it, so November wasn't the best time to try it out. I believe I should do it once more in the early spring or summer. Nevertheless, portraits do look fantastic. I wasn't certain if I was anticipating a more significant shift from the Q2. I discovered on the picture walk that my Leica Q2 cannot be replaced by the Q3 43. Traveling with two Leica cameras on top of my conventional ones didn't appeal to me much because I was constantly tempted to make my equipment lighter and smaller and wanted to discover a camera that could handle everything (portraits, landscapes, and wildlife photography). In terms of price, the two cameras are somewhat costly when purchased combined. About 6750 euros is the price of the Leica Q3 43. I was immediately informed by a colleague of mine who is also interested in photography that I could purchase three excellent lenses from a different manufacturer for that amount, which is accurate. If you prefer 50mm focal lengths, I can see the Leica Q3 43 being a fantastic camera for you. I'm tempted to purchase the Leica Q3 43, but I'm not going to do it just now. I would prefer to put my money aside for a new Leica camera that would better suit my needs. In the meantime, I'm trying to improve my Leica Q2's performance. As usual, the shooter needs to be improved, not the equipment. I'm hoping to get better at using the Q2 for portraiture.

Summary

The Leica Q3 43 offers a "normal" substitute for the company's full-frame compact wide-angle fixed lens. It has a great lens that produces amazing images, and its user interface is pleasantly photography-focused. Although it's focusing interface and video modes fall short of these incredibly high expectations, neither hinders the camera's primary function.

CHAPTER TWO
STARTING OFF WITH THE LEICA Q3

Unpacking and Initial Thoughts

It seems like the beginning of a singular, exhilarating, and breathtaking experience to take the Leica Q3 43 out of its box. The exquisite yet understated design of the box makes it stand out immediately. Although the box isn't overly large or hefty, it appears to have been meticulously constructed, as one could anticipate from a Leica brand. Even before you reach the camera, it feels sturdy and secure, which is a positive indication of quality. Everything within is arranged in a tidy group, each object easily accessible but secure. You can immediately tell that the packing process is not in a rush. Leica wishes to maintain the opulent experience they provide. When you take the Q3 43 out of its box, you can tell it's sturdy because it feels hefty. It has a pleasing ring that represents the high caliber of the camera's construction, but it is not overly hefty. It feels upscale because to the metal, yet secure and comfortable thanks to the side's silky grip. Even before you start shooting, you can see that this camera is designed to be enjoyable to use. Although not overly ostentatious, the camera's body has a smooth finish. It's elegant without being ostentatious. It is traditional in both appearance and feel in your hands. You feel as though you've just received a unique package because of the subtle yet elegant matte black hue and the exquisitely crafted Leica emblem on the front. One of the first things you notice is the 43mm f/2 APO-Summicron lens. Because it's compact, tidy, and understated, it blends in flawlessly with the camera's straightforward design. The aperture ring is smooth to the touch and applies the ideal amount of pressure, and the lens is well-made. It is evident from the lens's sense of accuracy that Leica didn't cut any corners. The fact that it's a fixed lens means you won't have to change lenses. It's excellent for daily shooting, headshots, and street photography.

The camera's rear has also been thoughtfully designed. The precise and bright 3.68-megapixel electronic viewfinder makes it easy to see what you'll see through the lens. The large touchscreen LCD comes to life with vibrant colors and fast reactions as you turn on the camera, and the viewfinder illuminates and is incredibly clear. As you switch settings, the tablet glides fluidly and without lag, making the experience simple to comprehend. Leica avoids providing unnecessary features or too many choices to keep things straightforward and user-friendly. The buttons and control knobs on the camera are positioned perfectly for ease of access. You can feel the accuracy of each adjustment when you adjust shutter speed, ISO, and aperture. You can feel a click to make sure you're making the right adjustments, and the dials are smooth. Because everything feels delibe rate, you have confidence that every shot will be precisely what you want it to be. Leica clearly prefers the tactile feel over digital menus and buttons, and the controls have an air of the past. You can tell right away that the Q3 43 was thoughtfully designed to feel good in your hands. It is tiny enough to be portable and has a sturdy feel rather than being flimsy or plasticky. Remarkably light for a full-frame camera, the camera is. For photographers who desire top-tier performance without the burden of a larger DSLR, this makes it ideal. Because of its versatility, this camera is easy to pack in your backpack. It also has a sturdy, long-lasting feel. So far, my impression of the Leica Q3 43 is nothing short of spectacular. It's a camera with minimal functions that let you concentrate on taking pictures. It is a camera that inspires creativity due to its superior performance and straightforward design. Every aspect of the camera, from the viewfinder's quality to the picture's aesthetic appeal, has been thoughtfully designed to provide an experience that extends beyond simple photography. It's all about capturing moments as beautifully and cleanly as possible.

Configuring Your Camera

First Step: Put the SD card and battery in

The first thing you must do before using your Leica Q3 43 is insert the SD card and batteries. Open the battery compartment on the bottom of the camera to accomplish this. Simply slide the box cover open carefully to position the battery. To ensure there are no power issues throughout the shoot, it is crucial to ensure that it is securely fastened. Make sure the ring snaps into position after inserting your SD card into the same slot. Keep in mind that high-performance SD cards are compatible with the Leica Q3 43. Select a UHS-II card if you want better write speeds, particularly when shooting large files or movies. When they are both inside and you are prepared to utilize the camera, close the container.

Second Step: Turn the camera on

Now that your camera has power, it's time to turn it on. The camera's on/off dial is located near the shutter button in the top right corner. Simply turn it around to activate it. It will switch on, and the electronic viewfinder (EVF) and LCD screen will display the Leica logo. If you haven't already, this camera will also prompt you to select your time zone and language. Don't worry; this will just take a little time and is all a part of the setup procedure.

Third Step: Set Up the Fundamental Configurations

Turning on your camera will show you how to configure it. You will first be prompted to select a language. After selecting it, you will need to modify the date and time as well as specify the time zone. This aids your camera in accurately recording the time the pictures were taken. Touching the touchscreen allows you to rapidly switch between the options and adjust the settings. Your camera will be ready for use as soon as you complete this simple and quick first step.

Fourth Step: Modify the ISO Configuration

Once your camera is operational, it's critical to adjust your ISO settings according to the lighting conditions. On top of the camera, directly beneath the shutter button, is an ISO dial. You have the option of selecting your preferred ISO directly or allowing the computer to do it automatically. Generally speaking, bright environments are best suited for smaller ISO levels (such as 100 or 200), whereas gloomy environments are better suited for higher ISO settings (800 or more). The Q3 43 has excellent low-light performance thanks to Leica, so you can increase the ISO if necessary without experiencing significant image noise. To determine which ISO setting is appropriate for your shooting, experiment with the dial.

Fifth Step: Adjust the Shutter Speed and Aperture

One of the best advantages of the Leica Q3 43 is its full manual control. By adjusting the shutter speed and aperture, you can alter your shooting style. The lens itself controls the aperture with a transparent ring that clicks into place as you make adjustments. For headshots and other situations when you wish to blur the background surrounding your subject, the f/2 aperture provides a shallow depth of field. A dial on top of the camera allows you to adjust the shutter speed. You may easily set it to either record fast-moving subjects (use faster shutter speeds) or blur moving things (use slower shutter speeds). Because you have complete control over the exposure with these settings, you can be creative with your photographs.

Sixth Step: Modify the Autofocus Configuration

The Leica Q3 43 includes built-in phase-detection autofocus for speed and efficiency. However, you may wish to adjust the autofocus settings based on your needs. You can choose between manual focus, continual autofocus, and single-point autofocus using the focus mode slider on the back. For subjects that move quickly, Continuous Auto AF (C-AF) will ensure that the camera adjusts focus as the subject does. If you're filming a more stable scenario, the single-point autofocus ring (S-AF) will provide you with precise focus on your subject. You can also switch to manual focus, which gives you more creative possibilities, if you'd want to adjust the focus ring yourself.

Seventh Step: Personalize the Controls and Buttons

Leica understands that every shooter has different needs, which is why the Q3 43 allows you to personalize the function buttons on the camera. By giving the customizable buttons from the main menu specific responsibilities, you may fast adjust parameters like ISO, white balance, and shutter speed. This is especially useful if you frequently adjust settings while shooting. It will be more efficient and personalized to use the camera if you take the time to configure the buttons the way you prefer.

Comprehending the Buttons and Controls

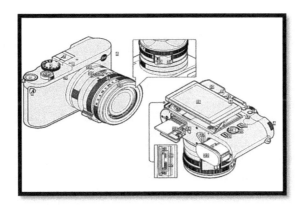

+ **The main switch:** the primary power switch that activates and deactivates the camera. Situated close to the camera's upper-right corner.
+ **The shutter button:** used for photography. While a full-press takes the picture, a half-press initiates autofocus.
+ **The Shutter-Speed Dial:** You have control over how long the shutter stays open by manually adjusting the shutter speed with this dial, which is located in the upper-right corner.
+ **Thumbwheel:** This handy function allows you to use your thumb to change settings like exposure compensation or aperture while holding the camera.
+ **The Thumbwheel Button:** This button, which is situated on the thumbwheel, offers more customization choices and makes a number of features easily accessible.
+ **Strap Lugs:** Used to fasten the camera strap, which enables you to carry your camera safely.
+ **Accessory Shoe:** You can connect external accessories like a flash, microphone, or other gadgets using the conventional hot shoe.
+ **Microphone:** This integrated microphone captures sound, which is helpful while filming videos.
+ **Self-timer LED/AF Assist Lamp:** In addition to helping with autofocus in low light, the LED illuminates when the self-timer is set.
+ **Viewfinder Eyepiece:** When you don't want to use the LCD screen, you gaze via the electronic viewfinder's (EVF) eyepiece to compose your photographs.
+ The Eye Sensor automatically switches the display from the LCD screen to the EVF when it detects that you are looking through the viewfinder.
+ **Diopter Wheel:** This wheel, which is adjacent to the viewfinder, modifies the focus of the viewfinder to suit your visual requirements.
+ **FN Button 1 (Function Button):** You can designate a certain function, such modifying focus modes or ISO, for easy access with this configurable function button.

- **The Function Button (FN Button 2):** You can pick a new quick-access function for your convenience when shooting with this additional customizable function button.
- **The LCD panel:** the camera's back screen, which is utilized for menu navigation, picture evaluation, and shot composition.
- Speaker Audio is played by the built-in speaker, including system notifications and the sound from a video recording.
- **LED Status:** This light shows the state of the camera's operation, including whether it is turned on, focusing, or processing a picture.
- **The "Play" button:** The playback mode button allows you to examine your films and pictures.
- **The Center Button:** This button, which is situated in the center of the directional pad, is frequently used to navigate through images during playback or to confirm menu selections.
- **Directional Pad:** You can swiftly change settings, explore the camera's menu, and navigate among images as they're playing back with the directional pad.
- **MENU Button:** This button brings up the camera's settings menu, where you may adjust various settings like image quality and white balance.
- **Compartment for Batteries:** the section that houses the camera's battery. To charge or replace the battery, it must be opened.
- **The Battery Release Lever:** When removing or replacing the battery, a tiny lever is utilized to free it from its compartment.
- **Tripod Thread:** This thread, which is found on the camera's bottom, enables you to fasten the camera to a tripod for steady images.
- **Slot for Memory Cards:** the slot for storing pictures and videos on your SD card. You may reach it from the camera's bottom.
- The camera's HDMI output enables you to show your images or videos on a TV or external monitor.
- **The USB-C output:** used to charge the camera or transfer data. Connecting to external devices for data backup or remote control is also useful.
- **Macro Function Alignment Point:** shows the precise location of the lens alignment to activate macro capabilities, enabling you to shoot close-up pictures.
- **Macro Ring:** The lens's movable ring that initiates and regulates the macro focus mode for up-close shots.
- **Focus Ring:** This ring gives you manual control over the lens's focus, allowing you to choose which areas of the image are crisp.
- **Aperture Ring:** Used to change the lens's aperture (f-stop), which regulates the amount of light that enters and gives you control over the depth of field in your images.
- **Thread Protection Ring:** This ring protects the lens threads from harm in the event that filters or other accessories are attached.
- **Lock Release AF/MF:** When switching focus modes, this button gives you the ability to lock and release the autofocus (AF) or manually focus (MF) settings.

⊥ The Focus Tab is a little tab on the lens that facilitates manual focus, improving control and grip while making adjustments.

About Display System

The pictures in the viewfinder and on the LCD panel are the same.

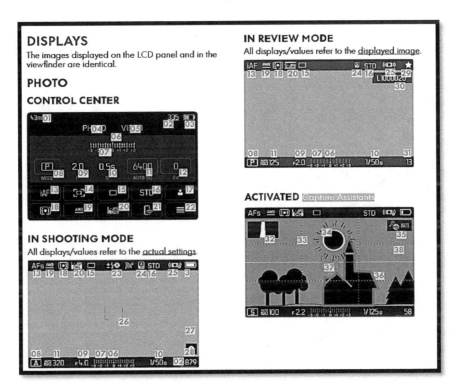

1. Focal length
2. Remaining storage capacity
3. Battery capacity
4. Menu section: PHOTO
5. Menu section: VIDEO
6. Light balance
7. Exposure compensation scale
8. Exposure mode
9. Aperture value
10. Exposure time
11. ISO Sensitivity
12. Exposure compensation value
13. Focus mode
14. Autofocus metering method

15. Shooting mode (Drive Mode)
16. Color rendering (Film Style/Leica Look)
17. User profile
18. Exposure metering method
19. White balance mode
20. File format/compression level/resolution
21. Leica FOTOS
22. Favorites menu / Main menu
23. Flash mode / Flash exposure compensation
24. iDR
25. Stabilization activated
26. AF Field
27. Bluetooth® (Leica FOTOS)
28. Geotagging
    ➢ Automatic storage of the shooting location (Exif data)
29. Icon for marked picture
30. File name
31. File number of the image shown
32. Histogram
33. Grid lines
34. Clipping identification of overexposed subject elements
35. Automatic magnification as focus assistance for manual focusing
    ➢ (3x or 6x magnification available)
36. Focus peaking
    ➢ (Identification of sharp edges in the object)
37. Level gauge
38. Display of cropped section size and position
    ➢ (Only visible for enlarged sections)

CHAPTER THREE
THE 60MP FULL-FRAME SENSOR: A GUIDE
Comprehending Image Quality and Resolution

You must understand sharpness and image quality if you want to get the most out of your Leica Q3 43. These two factors will have a significant impact on the photos you can take, so it's critical to understand how they interact and what settings you can adjust to achieve the greatest results.

Resolution

Resolution, which is typically expressed in megapixels (MP), is the number of pixels in an image. The camera controls how much information it can capture. The Leica Q3 43 has a 60-megapixel full-frame CMOS sensor. This sensor is capable of producing extremely high-quality images. This resolution allows the camera to capture a lot of detail, which is ideal for photojournalists who need crisp images for cropping, large prints, or detailed work. A higher megapixel count will result in a more detailed image. You can crop and zoom in on your photos and still get great clarity and sharpness. More resolution can also be beneficial, but there are drawbacks as well. Larger SD cards and greater computer space are required for editing because larger image files require more space. Higher resolution requires more processing power from your camera's CPU as well as from your editing software. Therefore, whether you're filming for the web or social media, you might not necessarily need to shoot at the highest quality. You can alter the size of your images to alter how they are utilized.

Image Quality

The camera's ability to capture details, colors, contrast, and noise is known as image quality. The camera's processing power, optics, and sensor all have an impact. While resolution plays a significant role in image quality, there are other factors to consider as well. The large, full-frame CMOS sensor of the Leica Q3 43 contributes to the creation of images with a broad dynamic range, clarity, and sharpness. As a result, the camera is able to capture more details in the shadows and highlights. This will help your photos appear more balanced and realistic, especially in poorly lit areas.

Depth and Accuracy of Color

The Leica Q3 43 is renowned for its rich, lifelike colors that aren't overly saturated. Leica lenses, like as the 43mm f/2 APO-Summicron, are designed to enhance the quality of your images by providing exceptional sharpness and great contrast, which keeps your details and colors sharp. From street photography to portraits, the Q3 43 is excellent for capturing a variety of topics.

Noise control

As the ISO (the camera's sensitivity to light) is increased, images may begin to exhibit more noise, particularly in low light. In contrast, the Q3 43's sophisticated sensor performs admirably at high ISO settings. This implies that even under challenging circumstances, you may take pictures in low light without noticeably increasing grain or losing clarity. Leica's noise reduction algorithms help to mitigate this issue, allowing you to capture sharper images without sacrificing the subtler details in the shadows.

The dynamic range

Dynamic range in photography refers to the camera's ability to capture both bright and dark areas without erasing any information. The Leica Q3 43 offers a broad dynamic range because to its full-frame sensor and strong image processing. This implies that you can still capture detail in both the dark and light areas of the picture when shooting in conditions that feature both deep shadows and bright highlights, such on a sunny day with a lot of contrast. Those that capture landscapes and scenes with dramatic lighting may find this very useful.

Compression and File Formats

File format options such as RAW and JPEG affect the size and quality of the images. Editing in RAW gives you additional choices. You may shoot in both RAW and JPEG formats with the Leica Q3 43. **Each of these file types has advantages and disadvantages in terms of image quality:**

- Because JPEG is a compressed file format, the camera reduces the size of the image to conserve space. This is ideal if you require a reduced file size and don't want to do a lot of post-processing. However, this compression can reduce the quality of the image, so you might need to cut it or make several alterations.
- Conversely, raw files are not compressed at all or barely marginally and retain all of the original data that the sensor recorded. This allows you a lot more latitude in post-processing because you may alter exposure, color, and white balance without compromising the image's quality. For experienced photographers who want the most control over their images, RAW files are the ideal choice because they are larger and occupy more space on your memory card and hard drive.

Lenses and the Quality of Images

The lens you use has a big impact on the quality of your photos. The 43mm f/2 APO-Summicron lens, which is known for its remarkable clarity and little distortion, is included as standard equipment with the Leica Q3 43. Your camera's lens has a big impact on image quality. The APO-Summicron ASPH lens, 43mm f/2. The lens that is included with the Q3 43 is Leica's most well-known lens. It is renowned for its stunning bokeh (out-of-focus areas) and flawless sharpness throughout the frame. Chromatic mistakes, or color fringes that might appear in scenes with a lot of contrast, are also greatly reduced by it. The lens's sophisticated optical design ensures that colors are accurate, details are sharp, and distortion is kept to a minimum, all of which improve the overall quality of the image. Since this lens is fixed, it cannot be changed. But because of its 43mm focal length, it can be used for landscapes, headshots, and even street photography. The Q3 43's ability to provide the advantages of a high-performance lens without compromising image quality is one of its key selling factors.

Selecting the Appropriate Image Quality Settings

By changing parameters like ISO, shutter speed, and aperture, you may enhance image quality in a range of lighting scenarios.

- **ISO:** Set your ISO as low as possible to preserve the highest possible image quality. However, the Q3 43 does well at higher ISO levels with minimal noise if you must increase it due to low light levels.
- **Aperture:** What size is it? For images when you want the backdrop to be blurry, a larger aperture, such as f/2, provides a shallow depth of field. To get the most sharpness across the frame, you might want to choose a narrower aperture (such as f/8 or f/11) for landscape photography.
- **Shutter Speed:** Adjust the shutter speed to manage motion blur. Slower shutter rates can be utilized for ring motion or artistic effects, while faster shutter speeds (such as 1/500 or faster) are best for taking crisp images of moving objects.

Comparing RAW and JPEG photography

Choosing to shoot in RAW or JPEG is one of the most crucial decisions you will have to make when using the Leica Q3 43. Your needs and the level of control you desire over your processed photos will determine which file format is ideal for you. Learn the differences between each format so you can select the one that best suits your photography style.

RAW File Type

RAW files give you the most editing choices because they are raw and contain all of the data that was captured by the camera's sensor. When you shoot in RAW, the camera does not process the image. Because the large file contains all of the sensor's raw data, you have complete control over the finished image after processing. Here's what to anticipate while shooting in RAW:

Benefits of RAW Shooting

- **Optimal Detail and Image Quality:** Because RAW files preserve all of the information that the sensor detects, the image has greater clarity and dynamic range. If you need to make adjustments after processing, this is quite beneficial. For instance, a RAW file is a far better option if you wish to restore highlights or edges that were cropped out of a JPEG. With the help

- Noise and restore of this app, you may alter an image's exposure, white balance, and even sharpness without sacrificing quality.
- **Greater Editing Control:** You have a lot more possibilities when it comes to photo editing with RAW files. You can adjust parameters like white balance, sharpness, color saturation, exposure, and even contrast without significantly lowering the quality because the camera hasn't processed the image yet (unlike with JPEG). If you want to conduct extensive editing or need to correct errors (such as exposure issues) after the fact, this is perfect.
- **Improved Efficiency in Low Light:** Using RAW files will provide you more post-processing options if you need to increase the ISO since you're shooting in low light. In order to eliminate characteristics that may have been lost in a JPEG.

The Drawbacks of RAW Shooting

- **Big file sizes:** Because RAW images are larger than JPEG ones, they occupy more space on your memory card and hard drive. Shooting in high quality or taking a lot of pictures might quickly fill up your storage.
- **Post-processing is necessary:** JPEGs do not require post-processing before sharing or copying, while RAW files do. However, because you have more editing choices in Adobe Lightroom or Photoshop, you will need to spend more time processing and modifying the files. Photographers may not want to utilize RAW if they want to use their images exactly as they are and don't want to alter them.
- **Slower Productivity:** Because RAW files are larger and require handling, your computer may take longer to open and modify them. This may cause the process to take longer, particularly if you are working with numerous images at once.

The JPEG format

JPEG is a processed and compressed format. The camera is configured to use contrast, sharpness, and white balance automatically. JPEG is a preferable file format for daily use. It requires no post-processing, is easy to store, and requires minimal room. **When shooting in JPEG, you should be aware of the following:**

Benefits of JPEG Photography

- **A smaller file size:** The fact that JPEG files are so much smaller than RAW data is one of its many advantages. Through processing and compression, it reduces the file size, allowing you to save more images on your memory card. This is the ideal choice if you're taking a lot of pictures fast or if your phone isn't too large.
- **Post-processing is not necessary:** You can utilize a JPEG photo as soon as you snap it. The camera adjusts the exposure, white balance, and sharpness of the picture for you. JPEG is an excellent choice for photojournalists who wish to spend more time taking

pictures and less time editing. Whether you need results fast or are aiming for social media, JPEG is a hassle-free choice.

- **Quicker Workflow:** Because JPEG files are smaller, opening and editing them takes less time. If you are under time pressure to send images, they expedite the process because they require less processing than RAW files.

The drawbacks of using JPEG for photography

- **Limited Flexibility in Editing:** You can't make as many adjustments with JPEG as you can with RAW because it has already been processed. When you take the picture, the camera will have already established the settings for you, and the picture will retain those settings. For example, it's much more difficult to correct exposure or white balance issues after the fact if you shoot with them incorrectly. Any alteration to the photo will result in a slight reduction in quality.
- **Poorer quality of images:** Because JPEG files are compressed; they may lose some information from the original image. This may blur the image, particularly in the highlights and blacks. JPEG compression can also result in noticeable imperfections, particularly if the image has been heavily altered or further reduced for online usage.
- **Less Post-Processing Flexibility:** When it comes to JPEG files, you can make some adjustments, but not as many as you can with RAW files. Adjusting details like exposure or restoring highlights may result in noise or a noticeable decrease in image quality.

Which Is Better to Pick?

RAW works best if
- In post-processing, you want complete control over your photos.
- Why you need the freedom to change exposure, white balance, and sharpness because you're shooting in challenging lighting circumstances.
- You intend to crop your images or create huge prints without sacrificing quality.
- You have the resources and time to process the photos at a later time.

JPEG works best if
- You don't want to bother about storage and require reduced file sizes.
- You don't require a lot of post-processing because the lighting is perfect for your shots.
- You don't want to spend time editing photos; you want to share or print them quickly.
- You have to take pictures fast and don't have time to edit each one after the fact.

Option Hybrid: RAW + JPEG

The Leica Q3 43 has the ability to shoot both RAW and JPEG simultaneously. This can be a fantastic choice if you want the best of both worlds. In addition to JPEG files that are prepared for immediate use or rapid distribution, you also receive RAW's flexibility for significant adjustments or future-proofing. However, keep in mind that both types of photography will require additional space.

Controlling Storage and File Sizes

Understanding how to manage file sizes and storage is crucial when using high-resolution cameras like the Leica Q3 43. When shooting in RAW, the camera's 60-megapixel sensor creates large image files that might quickly consume storage space. Here are some tips for managing your files and ensuring that you have adequate space when shooting.

Comprehending File Sizes

- **RAW Files:** The size of a 60-megapixel RAW file from the Leica Q3 43 can vary from 50MB to 80MB per image, depending on the quantity of information and image complexity. This implies that you can quickly accumulate several gigabytes if you're shooting in RAW format all day.
- **JPEG Files:** On the other hand, compressed JPEG files can be substantially smaller. The typical JPEG file size for a high-resolution file, such as the one from the Leica Q3 43, is 10–20 MB per image. JPEGs are smaller and save more space, but they may lose quality due to compression, particularly if you edit them frequently.

Controlling Storage

- **Selecting the Best Memory Card**
  - **Storage Space:** You must ensure that your memory cards have adequate space due to the size of RAW data. When shooting in RAW, a 128GB or 256GB SD card is a smart place to start because it will store a lot of images without needing to be changed frequently. If you're taking a lot of pictures at once, you may need a larger capacity card (512GB or more).
  - **Speed:** Seek out SD cards with a fast write speed, such as UHS-II cards. These cards are faster for writing large files, such as RAW images. This eliminates the need for the camera to buffer quick photos or wait while saving the image. Missed shots can result from slow memory cards, particularly while shooting continually or experiencing ring bursts.
- **Using two card slots (assuming there are any)**
  - As a precaution, you can configure the Leica Q3 43 to automatically backup your images to both SD cards since it supports two of them. This lessens the chance of a faulty card causing image loss.
  - In addition, you can configure the camera to save JPEGs on one card and RAW files on another. With this configuration, you may access the JPEGs fast for sharing or evaluating. In contrast, the high-quality RAW files remain on a separate card for further editing.
- **Frequently Creating File Backups**
  - **External Drives:** Following each shoot, you should transfer your picture files from your memory card to an external hard drive or solid-state drive (SSD). Compared to

standard hard disks, solid-state drives (SSDs) are quicker and more durable. Large files can be stored there safely. If you want to back up all of your images, you might want to purchase a large SSD.

➢ **Cloud Storage:** A cloud storage service like Google Drive, Dropbox, or Adobe Creative Cloud may be a good option if you want to secure your files. In the event that your hard drive is stolen or damaged, cloud storage backs up your data in a new location. Due to the limited amount of free space, you might need to purchase a plan if you want to store a large number of photos on the cloud.

✦ **How to Arrange Your Files**

➢ **Folder Structure:** Create a folder structure on your hard drive (or cloud storage) to arrange your photos by date, location, or project. **One possible arrangement for your photos would be as follows:**

```
/2025/
/March/
/Street Photography/
/Portraits/
/Landscapes/
```

➢ **File Naming:** Give each of your image files a unique name. This makes it easier to find photographs fast and prevents misunderstandings. For example, you might insert a number, the date, and the shooting place in the picture like this:

```
2025-03-10_Paris_001.raw
2025-03-10_Paris_002.raw
```

➢ **Make Use of Keywords and Metadata:** In addition to grouping your photos by file name and folder, you can also include keywords and other metadata. This will make finding specific photographs easier in the future, particularly if you have a large image library.

✦ **File Size Reduction without Quality Loss**

➢ **Downsample RAW Files:** If you don't need to maintain the full 60-megapixel resolution for every shot, you can downsample RAW files to a reduced resolution after processing. This reduces the file size without sacrificing image quality.

- ➢ **Compression programs:** To reduce the size of your RAW files without sacrificing image quality, you can also employ lossless compression programs. This allows you to save space without sacrificing image quality.
- ➢ **Shoot in JPEG for Fast Results:** Because JPEG takes up less space, you might want to test shooting in this format if you're just taking images for fun. However, remember that JPEG editing is more difficult than RAW editing, particularly when it comes to adjusting the exposure, white balance, or sharpness.
- ⬦ **Eliminating Unwanted Documents**
  - ➢ **Prepare for the shot:** Before every shot, remove any unnecessary photos from your memory cards that have already been transferred to your computer. This ensures that there is maximum space on your cards for new images.
  - ➢ **Post-Shoot Cleaning:** After transferring your images, spend some time going through them and removing those that didn't work out as you had hoped duplicates, or blurry images. This creates space for new files and keeps your storage organized.

The BSI CMOS Sensor: An Overview

The Leica Q3 43's Backside Illuminated (BSI) CMOS sensor is one of its greatest features; it significantly enhances the camera's performance, particularly in low light. The advantages of this sensor can help you comprehend how it enhances the dynamic range, shooting possibilities, and overall image quality.

A BSI CMOS sensor: what is it?

The light-capturing components (photodiodes) of a BSI CMOS sensor are located on the rear of the sensor rather than the front, as is the case with most other types of image sensors. A typical CMOS sensor has photodiodes on the front, but circuitry such as wires and transistors block them. The light that can reach the photodiodes may have been restricted by certain designers, which could reduce the sensor's usefulness, particularly in low light conditions. of contrast, the photodiodes of a Backside Illuminated (BSI) sensor are located on the rear of the sensor, allowing light to reach them directly without interference from other electronics. This facilitates the sensor's ability to detect light, particularly in dimly lit areas.

Advantages of the Leica Q3 43's BSI CMOS Sensor

- ⬦ **Enhanced Low-Light Efficiency:** BSI sensors perform exceptionally well in low-light conditions because they are able to detect more light. The BSI CMOS sensor's ability to function well in low light is among its best features. Because the sensor allows more light to reach the photo diodes, the Leica Q3 43 can maintain higher image quality when shooting in low light. You'll notice increased clarity and less noise (grain) even with higher ISO settings. When photographing indoors, at night, or at dusk, this is really beneficial. This implies that you may use the Q3 43 to take crisp, detailed photos at higher ISOs without worrying about experiencing significant image loss. Whether you're shooting in difficult lighting circumstances, at night, or indoors with ambient lighting, the BSI sensor ensures that your images will have more dynamic range and clarity, particularly in the shadows.

- **Increased Dynamic Range:** Because BSI sensors have a wider light spectrum, they can detect features in both bright and dark environments. Leica Q3 43's BSI CMOS sensor will give your images a greater dynamic range. The camera can now capture a greater variety of details, from the brightest to the darkest areas of an image. For example, while photographing a picture with deep shadows and intense sunlight, a BSI sensor can retain more information in both areas. This is due to the fact that it preserves shadow detail and avoids overexposing the highlights. This is especially useful for scenes with a lot of contrast, such as those in street or landscape pictures. The BSI sensor makes it possible for the Q3 43 to capture images that are more balanced and realistic, even in difficult lighting situations.

- **Improved Clarity and Color Accuracy:** By enhancing color reproduction and overall clarity, BSI sensors provide images that are sharper and more colorful. Your images will have more accurate color and brightness since the BSI architecture allows light to reach the photodiodes. The Leica Q3 43's images are more realistic thanks to its enhanced sensor architecture, which produces richer tones and sharper highlights and shadows. The BSI sensor ensures that the colors in your photos are clear and vibrant even in low-light conditions since it can capture more light and produce superior images. The sensor helps ensure that the photos you take are realistic and true to life, whether you're shooting brightly colored scenery or portraits with complicated skin tones.

- **Noise Reduction at Higher ISOs:** The BSI sensor reduces noise in high-ISO and low-light images, making them crisper and cleaner. Among the many significant advantages of the BSI CMOS sensor is its ability to reduce image noise in low light and at higher ISO settings. Raising the ISO to compensate for low light on ordinary cameras frequently results in visible grain or noise. On the other side, the Leica Q3 43's BSI sensor has substantially better noise reduction, so you can shoot in low light with a significantly lower likelihood of getting unpleasant noise. As a result, you may take pictures at higher ISOs (800, 1600, or even higher) without sacrificing quality. You'll obtain crisper, more detailed images in low light, which is particularly useful for indoor photography, nighttime sessions, or any other situation when you need to capture more details in a dark space.

- **Better Autofocus Results:** Autofocus performs better with the BSI sensor, particularly in low light conditions. By more effectively collecting light, the BSI sensor improves photo capture and autofocus performance. Light is necessary for autofocus systems to properly lock on to a subject. More light reaching the sensor can improve the performance of the phase-detection autofocus system. This is particularly true in low-light conditions. In areas with less light, you can anticipate quicker and more precise focusing. For instance, when photographing in a dimly lit restaurant or on a nighttime street, the Q3 43 will be able to concentrate on your subject more rapidly and precisely. This will reduce the likelihood of focused errors or "hunting."

- **More Effective Use of Power:** The enhanced efficiency of the BSI sensor allows the camera to record better images while using less power. The Backside Illuminated design not only improves light sensitivity but also aids in power efficiency. The sensor can capture more light, which reduces the effort required by the camera to produce well-lit images. This may indicate a longer battery life. This implies that using higher ISOs or photographing in low light may result in a slightly longer battery life. If you want to shoot for extended stretches of time without worrying about the battery dying, this is useful.

CHAPTER FOUR

EVERYTHING ABOUT UTILIZING THE CAMERA

Excellent Overview of Leica Q3 43 Uses Compared to Fujifilm X100 VI

Twist the collar control to activate the camera. You are prepared to leave after a little more than a second. For devices with manual cables, the clicky shutter release has a threaded hole. The two primary exposure controls on the Q3 43 are the same: a shutter dial that clicks between 1/2000 and one second at single stops, and a lens aperture ring that clicks between f2 and f16 at third-stop intervals. Both the shutter dial and the aperture ring have A settings. The Q3 will be in Program Auto if you turn both to A. To utilize Aperture Priority, turn the aperture ring while keeping the shutter control on A. Do the opposite if you wish to use Shutter Priority. Turn both to full Manual in the interim. The thumb dial in the unmarked corner adjusts the exposure correction when the shutter dial is set to A. Alternatively, you can manually adjust the shutter speed by one-third using the thumb dial. Longer exposures up to two minutes can be set with the thumb dial while the shutter dial is set to one second. When two minutes have passed, you are in T mode, which involves opening the shutter with one dial press and stopping it with another. The quickest mechanical shutter speed at the faster end of the spectrum is 1/2000. In contrast to focus plane devices, where flash syncs are significantly slower, a leaf shutter allows you to sync a flash up to this speed. Yes, like other leaf shutters, it is quite quiet. It's perfect for taking street photographs because you can hardly hear it clicking. For the Q3 43, an additional automatic shutter is available that increases the peak speed to 1/16000 and enables you to use the widest aperture (f2) even in extremely strong lighting conditions. Be cautious, though, because the readout speed is somewhat slow, which could cause moving subjects to be distorted when using the electronic shutter. This holds true for every camera with 60 Megapixels.

Atop: To illustrate this, I've included a picture I took at 1/1600 panning using the motorized leaf shutter (left). The beach bungalows are, as you might assume, vertical. Examine the image on the right, which was taken with an electronic shutter and exhibits poor skewing but has the same exposure and motion speed. To be fair, I've noticed a similar effect with other cameras, such as the Sony A7R V. Use the electronic shutter only when the subject and the camera are motionless to prevent skewing marks. Another option is to use the mechanical leaf shutter alone; however in extremely light weather you won't be able to use the largest aperture (f2) because of its top speed of 1/2000. For instance, on my samples page, I had to utilize an automated shutter since I needed 1/8000 when using f2 in full sunshine at 100 ISO. In addition to having an internal ND filter that you can activate in the menus to add three stops of light before using the electronic shutter, the Fujifilm X100 VI also includes a leaf shutter that fires one stop faster at 1/4000. If the Q3 43 had also had an ND, that would have been excellent.

The back controls are also extremely basic. They are made up of two unmarked function buttons and a joypad with menu and play buttons on either side. Press and hold either function button to modify its operation. The thumbwheel on top and the buttons inside the joypad function in the same way. If the Spot, Field, or Zone focusing region is activated, you can shift the point of focus on the frame using the touchscreen or the joypad. Additionally, you can touch the AF region while using the viewfinder to move it. Left-eyed users should exercise caution, though, as your nose may accidentally move it. For this reason, I would have preferred a joystick. You can't have everything, though, because the X100 VI only has a joystick and no joypad. The user interface also reflects the simple, clean controls. A brief menu with exposure details and easy access to common settings such as AF mode, metering, drive, white balance, quality, and Film Style will appear when you push the menu button once. You can move about and make sure with the tablet or joypad. Six pages of options appear when you hit the Menu button once more. By doing this, the camera's options are reduced compared to some modern cameras. The composition is same; the Q3 43 shares the same screen and viewfinder as the Q3. With 5.76 million dots and a 0.76x zoom in 3:2, that is a large and crisp electronic viewfinder. It looks fantastic in real life, however like many high-quality EVFs, the resolution will decrease when the camera is autofocusing. Compared to the Q3 43, the Fujifilm X100 VI's 3.69 million dot viewfinder is smaller and less detailed.

The Q3 43 is unquestionably superior in terms of electronics, but if you'd prefer, the Fujifilm does have a mixed optical picture. The Q3's 1.8 million-dot, 3-inch screen is set on a mechanism that can tilt up by nearly 90 degrees for easier waist-shots or down by roughly 45 degrees for better sight when held overhead. It's a little unusual that it doesn't fold up all the way to a square, but it functions great. The Micro HDMI and USB C connectors are hidden behind a plastic flap on the left side. There are no headphones or mic connectors, although the USB C port will purportedly function with some USB C mics in the future. You can connect an external recorder to the HDMI port, charge the battery using the USB port, or operate the camera remotely using the USB port. A tripod pin that aligns with the optical plane is located below. It has slots for a card and a battery on either side. A single SD slot is visible when the card slot door clicks forward and opens. Either trying to fit two slots in or adding some built-in memory as a backup would have been excellent for the price. The majority of cameras of this size have just one slot. That would be more reassuring to me for one-time occasions like weddings. The battery is simultaneously popped out by turning a handle, and with one more push, it can be tossed out entirely. Thus, the room door is a component of the battery. It is, as anticipated, the same BP-S CL6 as the Q3, which is reportedly good for roughly 350 shots under CIPA conditions. In my experiments, it frequently outlasted the X100 VI battery. If you dislike the concept of traditional USB charging, the Q3 43 also has a wireless charging pad accessory. The model number is etched adjacent to a flash hotshoe that is situated on top of the body. Flashes can be synced up to 1/2000, as I said earlier, but only 1/4000 on the X100 VI. Nevertheless, they are still significantly quicker than focal plane sync speeds. One of the Q3 43's most intriguing features is the lens. It is the first new lens in the Q line since its release in 2015, in addition to being a completely new optical design from Leica. This variant features three rings on the barrel, just like the original 28mm model. Nearest to the front is the aperture ring. It has a "A" option for automated control and moves in one-third steps from f2 to f16. In the center is the manual focusing ring. It stops hard at infinity and just over 60 cm (2 feet) after turning quite effortlessly.

The range of sharpness at f4, 8, 11, or 16 is indicated by a depth of field scale that is adjacent to the distance markers. This simplifies zone-focusing. At the final focusing point, the camera rapidly enlarges the screen and employs focus peaking to help you even more while you manually adjust the focus. Your thumb will naturally land on a tab with a little button on it that allows you to lock the camera into focusing while you hold the lens in your left hand. Holding down this button, rotate the focusing ring slightly past infinity to enter the AF position. Until you press the tiny button once more and switch the lens back to manual settings, AF locks the focusing ring in place. Initially difficult to use, the button functions flawlessly. Either manually or automatically, the camera will focus down to a distance of roughly two feet (60 cm). However, you may put the camera in macro mode, which expands the range to 60 to 27 cm, by twisting the third ring next to the camera body. A new distance scale is revealed when you rotate this ring, which causes the entire optical group to travel outward. However, the camera will still require you to hit the AF button at the end in order for it to autofocus. It's interesting to see that the aperture actually closes by one stop to f2.8 while the Q3 43 is in macro mode. The diaphragm system truly closes to f2.8 regardless of where the aperture ring is placed between f2 and f2.8, so this is more than just a shift in the amount of light it collects. Until you close it still farther, it will remain at 2.8. As you can see, this implies that bokeh blobs in macro mode will have a geometric shape even at the widest aperture. Additionally, as was previously mentioned, using filters with the kit's oblong hood will be challenging due to the optical group moving outward. Next up, the Q3 43 features the same high-quality lens selections and 60-megapixel full-frame CMOS sensor as the original Q3. If 60 Megapixels is too much, you can shoot in 14-bit DNG RAW, 8-bit JPEG, or both. You can record in four different methods, but there are no compression choices.

Leica makes use of the many cropping choices provided by the high resolution by including ring settings for 60, 75, 90, 120, and 150mm in the Digital Zoom menu. The crops get worse as you adjust the settings. The quality simply decreases as the cuts grow smaller because the camera doesn't attempt to upscale. You can also alternate between these settings while composing, displaying the area in a smaller frame. There are benefits and drawbacks to this approach. One advantage is that you will be able to view subjects outside the frame, similar to a range finder, which will allow you to adjust the composition or prepare. The issue is that when the frame size decreases, it becomes more difficult to organize properly. I wish there was a way to simply fill the frame or EVF with the active area rate instead. In the selections, I might have overlooked it. The natural image can capture at full 60-megapixel quality in either case if you use a 43mm lens. If you select the 60mm size, it decreases to 31 Megapixels. At 75mm, the quality reaches up to 20 Megapixels. At 90mm, 14 Megapixels are utilized. At 120mm, the sharpness has decreased to eight Megapixels. Lastly, only five Megapixels remain in the 150mm range, the smallest, after the enormous cut. When viewing the entire image on YouTube or social media posts, you can still see that much information, but you are unable to enlarge it further. When recording, remember that DNG files will include the entire 43mm view, but with automatic post-production cropping instructions. However, most programs allow you to return to the wider view if you want. To be honest, I hardly ever desired to utilize any of the compressed modes because I felt that the 43 focal length was so versatile. Of course, if I wanted to, I could always grow crops in post-production.

We may examine noise across the ISO range with the Q3 43's lowest sensitivity setting of 50 ISO. I'll try the image processing and noise reduction technique using JPEGs from the camera and zoom in by 600% to see if anything changes. Watch my review video up there to see it in its entirety. I'll include the Fujifilm X100 VI on the right at the same resolution because I was also interested in it for scholarly purposes. I shifted the camera forward somewhat to compensate for the larger lens and to match the subject size on the frame. It will be intriguing to observe how the degree of detail varies along the range, even if the sensor is smaller and has less sharpness. The X100 VI's base setting, 125 ISO, which is its lowest extended sensitivity setting, is used in two of the pictures on this page. While Fujifilm's NR provides comparable detail at 800 ISO, Leica's NR provides comparable detail at lower ISOs. Both of them were then photographed at 200 ISO, and now at 400 ISO. At 1600 ISO, both cameras begin to exhibit increased noise, and both modes thereafter gradually worsen.

Leica Q3 43 at 6400 ISO   Fujifilm X100 VI at 6400 ISO

Atop: 6400 ISO is selected on both cameras. Because it displays more speckles, it's interesting to see the point at which the noise reduction technologies on both cameras fail. From 12800 ISO onward, Fujifilm's strategy appears to completely shift, whilst Leica's noise pattern deteriorates with time. When both cameras are on maximum sensitivity, they don't look very good. You can choose between single and continuous autofocus modes, or you can let the camera select the autofocus mode that works best for the subject. As previously stated, the viewfinder quality will momentarily deteriorate when continuous autofocusing is engaged. Zone, field, and spot AF areas allow you to zoom in or out as needed, and Multi-Field allows the camera to figure it out. The next feature is tracking, which allows you to place a frame over a subject and track it by holding down half of the shutter button. The frame begins in the center by default, but you can move it about with the joypad or touchscreen. After repositioning it, you can optionally select whether it returns to the center or the final active location. Although the AF motor itself performs best in slow motion, it can really track a subject around the frame seamlessly. If the topic is a human, select the Eye, Face, or Body identification option. By placing squares over both eyes and emphasizing the one that is closer, it gives the impression that the individual is wearing spectacles. Lastly, you can expand the list to include animal recognition. However, if you have pets other than cats and dogs, your results can differ because Leica only discusses common pet categories, not specific ones.

Let's now attempt to focus in real life. We'll begin with a spot area in the center of the frame and the single AFS mode. The bottle is inside the typical focusing range of the camera. You can observe how quickly and effortlessly the camera refocuses when the aperture is wide open. However, it performs less well, at least in our configuration, when set to constant AFC. Since the camera feels faster and safer in single AFS mode, I personally prefer it to continuous AF. However, I only experienced problems focusing when the subject was outside of the regular range when I used it normally. Changing to macro mode made fixing that simple. When I perform my concentration breathing test from infinity to 60 cm, which is the typical range, the view likewise becomes slightly larger. Any shaking in images, films, and compositions can be fixed with the lens's optical image stabilization ring. In my tests, it only appeared to function with a half-press, regardless of whether this was set to Auto or On. This is an illustration of the slowest shutter speed of < that I was able to maintain while using OIS. However, the image I captured at 1/4 of a second wasn't too terrible. The OIS-containing ≽ sample will remain on the left. I'll show you the same exposure on the right, but it's lot less visible without OIS. To capture a sharp shot with the Q3 43 that day without stabilization, I actually had to set the shutter speed to 1/125. This indicated that four to five stops were actually being compensated for by the OIS. To make the most of the incredibly high-resolution sensor, it is therefore a helpful feature.

Atop: I'm going to start studying the optical quality now. I'll begin with a far landscape image that is angled so that characteristics extend to the boundaries. As always, I find that testing lenses on a real-world distant subject is more useful for evaluating lens quality than taking close-up pictures of a chart. The aperture is wide open at f2 in this Q3 43. The details are already rather obvious and well-corrected if you take a closer look in the middle at 600%. For a detailed comparison of all the variants, see my video review at the top. Although f2.8 will give your ring a little more strength if you're really interested in pixel peeping, this lens performs admirably wide open for the most part. Up to f5.6, the best quality remains constant as the aperture is further reduced. However, contrast and sharpness begin to somewhat diminish at f8. This is more apparent at f11, while the overall sharpness is much less apparent at f16, the shortest aperture, due to diffraction. To get the best shots, I would aim to shoot between f2.8 and 5.6 if depth of field isn't an issue. Return to the example of f2, and notice how much sharper it is. Next, proceed to the distant corner, where sharpness won't be significantly impacted. The corner sharpness improves as I gradually reduce the aperture, reaching its maximum at f5.6. However, diffraction softens the corners at narrower apertures.

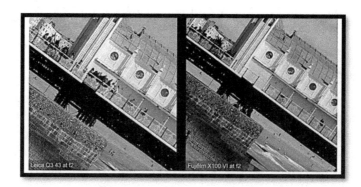

For fun, let's return to f2 in the center of the frame and examine the Fujifilm X100 VI on the right and the Q3 43 on the left. In this instance, both are blown up by the same amount, but the details are less evident because the Fujifilm has a larger lens. Although there are a few possible differences, like as resolution, sensor size, and focal length, it is evident that the X100 VI lacks the bite and final detail of the Q3 43 when it is wide open. The Leica's lens and sensor combination is obviously capturing much finer details, which is to be expected given the price and specifications, but the Fujifilm can perform better when the aperture is closed. I thought it would be interesting to examine how each camera photographed the same image in high contrast greyscale mode, though, as it's not all about examining minute details.

Atop: The Leica Q3 43 in its Monochrome High Contrast Film Style is visible on the left.

Atop: the Fujifilm X100 VI with the digital red filter is shown on the right in the ACROS film simulation. I prefer the red filter effect on the X100 VI sample on the right since it makes the blue sky darker. However, I believe they both have a similar appearance overall. Which is your favorite?

44

Atop: These are the color versions from both cameras, both in their default settings, for your amusement. These JPEGs were taken directly from the camera. The difference is more noticeable here because the X100 VI's basic Provia simulation displays stronger contrast and greater saturation. Although I appreciate Provia's punchiness, I've always felt that it was a little too potent for a typical profile. I think the Leica's typical profile on the left looks more natural, but as usual, these are simply personal preferences, and there are many more profiles available for both cameras. For instance, the Fotos app on the Leica allows you to select from a wide variety of profiles.

The Leica Q3 43 then locked on to me in a portrait test at f2, and when I zoomed in for a closer look, I could discern characteristics that were as distinct as those of the best Sony GM lenses I had tried. There is still a lot of blur and separation in the background, and there is a pleasant reduction in sharpness between the focus region and the rear of my yard, even if the 43 f2 doesn't have as short of a depth-of-field as the 50 1.4 prime. Taking close-up portraits is a great use for the 43 f2 lens.

The X100 VI will be on the right, and the Q3 43 on the left. I'll be the same distance away from both, and they'll both be set at f2. It's intriguing to observe how differently they evaluate skin tones and white balance under the identical lighting circumstances. Once more, the Leica appears more realistic in this instance. The X100 VI's larger field of vision and smaller sensor also result in significantly less background blur than you might expect. My face is now distorted since this is getting too close for a 35-equivalent lens. You'll see a bit more blurring in the background if I get a little closer to the Fujifilm to about match the subject size. As you might anticipate from a DSLR with a lens and sensor, the Q3 43 offers a lot more information than the landscape view.

Atop: Here is my ornament test, which was taken with the Q3 43 at its closest focusing distance and with the aperture wide open (f2.8 in macro mode) for a more sobering look at bokeh and background blur. The blobs appear largely clean with only a faint outline at this aperture, but at the largest aperture, you can see that they lack any curvature. As you can see, many of them are now depicted as nine-sided forms, which stand in for the now-emerging nine-bladed diaphragm system. The aperture blades are now causing the blobs in the far corner to organically extend. Therefore, even with the ring set to f2, the advertised f2.8 aperture in macro mode is more than just a shift in exposure. Even with the setting all the way up, the bokeh isn't smooth in this mode because the shutter system has actually closed up a bit.

Atop: I've included one of my test photographs taken at f2, at the very close end of the usual focusing range, just to show you how the two images compare. As one might anticipate at the widest aperture, the bokeh blobs are curved. Use the standard focusing range if you don't want nine-sided bokeh blobs. Let's return to my macro ornament test now. Since f2.8 is still the highest aperture, moving the aperture ring from f2 to f2.8 has no effect. At f4, though, the blobs become more uniform and smaller throughout the frame. As the aperture shrinks and the geometric shape becomes more apparent, the blobs continue to get smaller.

Let us now examine the X100 VI with an aperture of f2 on the right and the sample with an aperture of f2.8 on the left. Once again, the ornament and the blobs are smaller due to the larger lens of the Fujifilm, but at the widest aperture, they are at least round because this image was taken from the same distance.

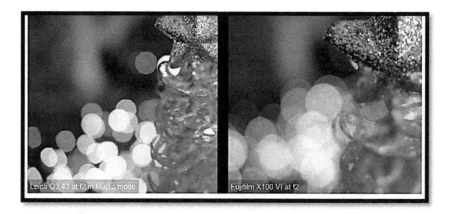

Atop: In order to take advantage of the X100 VI's unique ability to focus closer, we'll swap out the image on the right with the one at its closest focusing distance, where the blobs and ornament are larger. Since the diaphragm system is still out of the way and the blobs remain clean and colorless, I would say that they are also good here. If you can take advantage of the subject's proximity, this is a positive outcome. To find the maximum reproduction of the Q3 43's lens, I placed my ruler as near to the camera as it will focus in macro mode, which is 168mm across the frame. Even at f2.8, the details are crisp and clear right down to the edges, which isn't that large in macro terms. In contrast, the Fujifilm X100 VI's tighter focus allows it to capture 94mm across the frame; however, the edges become less sharp until the lens is closed down to approximately f5.6. Before I finish, I wanted to briefly discuss video. The Q3 43 can record decent-looking recordings up to 8k, although most users will likely capture video. The menus also offer a wide range of compression settings, including LongGop, All-i, and even internal ProRes, albeit the latter is limited to 1080 60p. The Q3 43 was used to record this 1080p 25p video clip, which does not crop the field of vision. It enables you to compare the variety and quality. With the same coverage as previously, now in 1080p at 50p. The next setting is 1080 100p, which records with sound and at standard speed so that you can slow it down in post-production. Look at the lesser quality and the crop. To demonstrate how much more ground it covers, let's now return to 1080 at 25p. After that, we'll move to 4K at 25p, which has a tighter crop than 1080 at 100p but records more data. The crop remains the same in 4k 50, however you may notice a decrease in clarity. Last but not least, there is 8k 25p, which has the same crop as 4k but more detail. See how I can maintain the 4K clarity while making this twice as large on a 4K timeline. Take a test that requires you to focus. The Q3 43 can shoot in 4K if it has continuous autofocus and a single spot area in the center of the frame. At least with the default settings, it's not the most responsive or certain of its outcome, which makes it somewhat reminiscent of Fujifilm's movie focusing, which occasionally falters as well. Why don't you follow your face? Once more, the AF method is not ideal for subjects that are constantly moving because it takes a while to react whether I move closer or farther away. However, you can see that the system will get the proper focus and provide the active rendering I demonstrated in my previous portrait testing if you wait a moment for it to catch up. Last but not least, wait as I demonstrate some rolling shutter testing. Since 1080 25p has the least degree of skewing, I'll start with that. The same is true for 1080 at 50p, which remains pleasant. However, because the readout is slower at 4K 25p, the skewing from the rolling shutter is clearly visible. For 8k, the same holds true. It's intriguing to note that skewing significantly decreases when switching to 4k 50p because the readout is faster, but this could also indicate that there is less information.

CHAPTER FIVE
ABOUT SUMMILUX 28MM F/1.7 LENS
Features of the Focal Length of 28mm

- **Broad Field of View:** Your field of view is significantly less with a standard lens, such as a 50mm or 35mm, than with a 28mm lens. For vast scenarios where you want to capture more of the environment, including landscapes, skyscrapers, or even street photographs, this wider angle is perfect. Its wide perspective gives you the impression that you are actually in the scene you are filming.

- **Ideal for Environmental Portraiture:** The 28mm isn't just for landscapes and structures; you can use it creatively to capture portraits in their natural environments. When you take a picture of someone in their natural environment, you can clearly depict both the person and their surroundings. The fact that a 28mm lens doesn't alter the subject's features as much as a 24mm or 21mm lens does is important in this situation.

- **Very Little Distortion:** Compared to ultra-wide lenses, a 28mm lens eliminates the majority of the distortion at the frame's edges. Because of this, it's a fantastic option for photographing people and structures without the too curved straight lines that you might find with lenses larger than 28mm.

- **Outstanding Low-Light Capabilities:** Many lenses in the 28mm range have high apertures, such as f/1.4 or f/2.8, which are excellent in low-light conditions. You can still snap bright, clear photos even under poor lighting conditions. It's an excellent tool for nighttime street photography and low-light situations.

- **Small and light:** A 28mm lens has the advantage of often being lightweight and compact. This facilitates portability, particularly when traveling or exploring. For those who desire a broad view without making their camera too large, this lens is fantastic.

- **Excellent for Street Photography:** For street photographers, the 28mm focal length is often a favorite since it provides the perfect mix between getting near to subjects and still being able to capture their surroundings. It allows you to remain close to the action without being overly close, while also providing a broad enough perspective to grasp the scene's core idea.

- **Clarity and Sharpness:** Even when taken wide open, 28mm lenses are generally regarded as having excellent sharpness. If the small details are important to you, a good 28mm lens may capture incredibly sharp photographs, even at the frame's corners.

- **Field Depth:** Due to its broader field of view, a 28mm lens has a deeper depth of field than a telephoto lens. More of the scene will be in focus as a result. This is useful when you want the backdrop and center to remain crisp. When you simply want to display one subject, you can still achieve lovely bokeh (blurring of the backdrop) with a larger aperture, such as f/1.4.

- **Adaptable to Various Kinds of Photography:** The 28mm lens performs admirably across the board in terms of various shooting styles. It can handle any type of photography, whether you're taking street scenes, cityscapes, landscapes, or portraits. It is just broad enough to inspire your imagination, but not too broad that it is unusable.

- **Original Composition:** The 28mm focal length allows you to create imaginative pictures. Because the view is larger, you can experiment with elements in the background and center, leading lines, and empty space. Compared to standard focal lengths, it gives your photographs a more dynamic feel and helps you create intriguing, depth-filled images. Ultimately, a lens with a 28mm focal length is one that may be utilized for a wide variety of photographs. Its broad field of vision, balanced perspective, and user-friendliness make it an excellent choice for photographers who wish to capture more images without sacrificing portability or image quality. When shooting close-up street photographs, wide views, or urban scenes, the 28mm lens offers a decent balance of distortion and wide-angle coverage that looks natural.

Lens Performance: Distortion, Bokeh, and Sharpness

Three important aspects that are commonly discussed when evaluating a lens's performance, particularly one like the 28mm, are sharpness, bokeh, and distortion. **Numerous factors influence how the lens produces your images and can significantly impact your creative decisions.**

- **Sharpness using a focal length of 28 mm:** The 28mm lens is renowned for its exceptional sharpness, particularly when paired with a premium lens like those found in Leica's product line. **Here's how it operates:**
  - **Center Sharpness:** The center of the frame is typically extremely sharp, even when shooting wide open. At f/2.8 or f/1.4 (depending on the lens), you'll notice that subjects in the center of the frame appear sharp, as do minute details like textures. The fact that sharpness is usually maintained in the center of the shot with little loss is one of the reasons 28mm lenses are so popular among street and landscape photographers.
  - **Edge and Corner Sharpness:** You might notice that the edges and corners of your frame soften a little while shooting wide open, particularly at lower f-stop values like f/1.4 or f/2. As is common with wide-angle lenses in general, the lens finds it more difficult to maintain flawless clarity over the entire frame as the angle increases. However, the edges become considerably sharper and the sharpness is more uniform from the center to the corners of the picture when you stop the lens down to about f/5.6 or f/8.
  - **Aperture and Sharpness:** When stopped down, the 28mm lens often performs admirably. This means that for crucial pictures that require the highest level of sharpness (like landscape shots), you should reduce the aperture to f/5.6 or f/8. These apertures produce a sharp image in the center and along the edges, making them ideal for larger images.
- **Bokeh with a focal length of 28 mm:** Bokeh refers to the quality of the out-of-focus areas in a picture, especially the way the background is portrayed. Compared to longer focal lengths like the 50mm or 85mm, bokeh is less obvious with the 28mm lens. This is

due to the 28mm lens's broad field of view, which maintains the majority of the scene in focus. However, there are still a few significant aspects to it:

- ➤ **Background Blur:** Even while focusing on close-up subjects, you can achieve some background blur at larger apertures, such as f/1.4 or f/2. However, the blur isn't as smooth or obvious as it would be with larger lenses designed for photography due of its wide field of vision. The 28mm lens is softer and more subdued, highlighting the foreground with a gently faded background.

- ➤ **Bokeh Shape:** The bokeh's shape is greatly influenced by the lens's aperture blades. If your lens has rounded aperture blades, the out-of-focus regions (such as background light spots) will appear smoother and more rounded. This ultimately improves the bokeh's appearance and appeal. However, some 28mm lenses, particularly those with fewer aperture blades, might make bokeh appear sharper. This implies that the background may not be as seamless.

- ➤ **Excellent for Bokeh:** Due to its broad field of view, which makes it challenging to distinguish a subject from a fuzzy backdrop, the 28mm lens isn't typically selected for its bokeh effect. You can still get good shots, though, if you position your subject closer to the background. This is frequently useful in street or outdoor portrait photography when you want some blur but still need background information.

- ✦ **Distortion with a focal length of 28 mm:** The way the lens alters the shape of objects in the frame—mostly those on the sides or corners—is known as distortion. Depending on your shooting technique and the lens' construction, you may notice distortion when using a 28mm lens.

  - ➤ **Barrel Distortion:** Straight lines, particularly those near the edges of the frame, begin to bend outward when using a wide-angle lens, such as the 28mm, giving the impression that the image is bulging. That is known as "barrel distortion." A slight barrel distortion may occasionally be seen at 28mm, but it is less obvious than with ultra-wide lenses like 24mm or 21mm. In most shooting situations, this slight distortion is not evident unless you're shooting straight lines, such as architectural shots, directly against the boundaries.

  - ➤ **Distortion Control:** Good 28mm lenses, such as those made by Leica, frequently have excellent lens control, thus in practical applications, barrel distortion can be negligible or even nonexistent. Many cameras, particularly digital ones, have built-in distortion correction capabilities, which further reduces the visibility of this type of lens defect.

  - ➤ **Perspective:** The 28mm lens has a tendency to exaggerate the rate of perspective, making objects near the camera appear larger and objects farther away appear smaller. This is something to be aware of. When taking photographs in the street or in the surrounding surroundings, you can get creative with this. However, if you don't want the distortion to make your subjects look strange, don't place them too close to the edges.

An overview

+ **Sharpness:** Generally excellent, with sharp features in the middle, while the edges may get a little softer. The edge becomes much sharper when you stop down.
+ **Bokeh:** At wide apertures, you can still get a beautiful background blur, especially with close subjects. It's subtle and soft, not as noticeable as longer focal lengths.
+ **Distortion:** Not as bad as with ultra-wide lenses, but there is some barrel distortion. High-quality lenses have very little distortion, which is frequently fixed by the camera or software.

Overall, the 28mm lens performs admirably in terms of distortion control, bokeh, and clarity. For those who desire a large field of vision without sacrificing image quality, this makes it an excellent option. It records crisp, clear images with minimal distortion, making it ideal for taking pictures of large vistas, cityscapes, and outdoor scenes.

Making Effective Use of the Macro Mode

Comprehending Macro Mode

You can focus on objects that are extremely close to your lens when in macro mode, typically at distances that are significantly closer than the typical focusing distance. **The 28mm and most other lenses have a close-focus range, but true macro lenses allow you to capture lifelike images or even expand objects beyond their true size.**

+ **True Macro vs. Close Focus:** With a 1:1 reproduction ratio, the object you're photographing appears on the camera's sensor at its actual size. Although some lenses, such as your 28mm, can focus up close, they might not have a 1:1 ratio, so your subject won't appear life-sized in the picture. However, they can still provide incredible close-up clarity.
+ **Focusing Distance:** When utilizing macro mode, you must be extremely near to the subject—typically only a few inches. Although this can occasionally make lighting and composition more challenging, the advantages of getting close-up shots of little objects, textures, and minute details may outweigh the drawbacks.

Manage Your Field of View

One of the most challenging aspects of macro photography is managing the depth of field (DOF). The image's focus may be extremely shallow when you're concentrating on tiny objects. This implies that the majority of your subject will blur together, with only a little section remaining sharp. **Here's how to deal with it:**

+ **Aperture Control:** To alter the depth of field and get more of your subject in focus, choose a smaller aperture (higher f-stop number), such as f/8 or f/11. While less light may reach the sensor as a result, more of the subject will remain in focus, which is useful when photographing little objects with lots of minute details.
+ **Focus stacking:** Taking multiple shots at different focus points and then combining them in post-processing to create an image with a much deeper DOF is known as "focus

stacking." This technique is useful if you need an even deeper depth of field, particularly for small objects with a lot of surface detail.

Employ Appropriate Lighting

Macro photography requires adequate lighting, but because you're working with small things, you also need to be able to manage the lighting so that specific areas of your subject aren't overly bright or create sharp shadows. **Here are some lighting strategies to improve your macro photos:**

- ✦ **Natural Light:** Soft natural light is frequently the greatest choice for a photographer when photographing close-up subjects. Early morning or late afternoon light is usually softer and more flattering to the ring when the sun is lower in the sky. However, unless you can spread the light out, it might not be the ideal because harsh noon light might create sharp shadows.
- ✦ **Artificial Light:** If you're shooting indoors or in low light, you may need to utilize an external flash or a specialized macro light. Ring lights are popular among photographers because they illuminate your subject directly and eliminate shadows. Try using a filter while using a flash to soften the light and prevent strong hues.
- ✦ **Reflectors:** By bouncing light back onto the subject, reflectors help fill in shadows and provide more uniform illumination for the picture. A plain white piece of paper or fabric will do just fine.

Make Your Camera Stable

Macro images can be a touch wobbly because you're working with such tiny focus planes and frequently taking them by hand. **Stabilizing the camera is essential because even slight movements might affect how crisp your image is:**

- ✦ **Tripod:** One of the greatest ways to maintain camera stability and ensure perfect focus is with a sturdy tripod. When using a smaller aperture (higher f-stop) and requiring a shorter shutter speed to compensate for the lack of light, this is particularly useful.
- ✦ **Remote Shutter or Timer:** If you're using a tripod, be sure your camera doesn't shake when you push the shutter button. The timer feature or a remote shutter release can be used for this.
- ✦ **Lens Stabilization:** If you're shooting with your hands, using a lens with image stabilization (IS) can assist reduce the impacts of camera shake. However, be cautious to switch off the stabilization while using a tripod, as this can occasionally result in fuzzy images.

Select the Appropriate Focus Mode

Macro photography requires you to concentrate on extremely fine details, which can be challenging because even slight movements might cause you to lose focus. **How to handle it:**

- ✦ **Manual Focus:** Many photographers prefer to use manual focus when shooting in macro mode because it allows them to have more control over the focus point's location. With manual focus, you may gradually shift the focus ring around until you get sharp features exactly where you want them.

- **Focusing:** Advanced focusing mechanisms found in some new cameras and lenses can be helpful when taking macro images. But be aware that lens autofocus can often struggle with little subjects, particularly if you are extremely close to them. Choose a single-point point mode if you're using autofocus, and concentrate on the most crucial aspect of your subject.
- **Focus Peaking:** To make the regions in focus stand out, some cameras have a feature called focus peaking that tints them with a color. When utilizing manual focus for macro photography, this can be a huge assist in getting sharp focus.

Write with Care

Composition is equally crucial in macro photography as it is in other forms of photography. The objects you're utilizing are small, so you have to be quite careful about how you fill the photo and frame it.

- **Rule of Thirds:** This guideline will assist you in choosing the best location for your subject. Because the subject is small, it's usually ideal to keep it off-center to add more movement to the picture.

How to Optimize the f/1.7 Aperture

- **The Shallow Depth of Field: Accept It:** The f/1.7 aperture has the advantage of having a relatively tiny depth of focus. This allows you to isolate your topic from the background, which is ideal for product photographs, portraits, and other scenarios where the subject needs to be kept apart. Approach your topic and concentrate on their face or the most significant feature. After that, see how the background becomes a gentle, even blur. **Pro Tip:** If you are closer to the subject and use a larger aperture (such as f/1.7), the depth of field will be stronger. There is a noticeable contrast between the sharp subject and the fuzzy background.
- **Benefit from Low Light:** The large aperture of f/1.7 allows light to reach the sensor. As a result, you may take pictures in low light without increasing the ISO or lowering the shutter speed. This is particularly useful for indoor shots, night scenes, or any other scenario where there is inadequate illumination without sacrificing image quality. **Pro Tip:** You can utilize faster shutter speeds even in darker conditions if you shoot at f/1.7. This will help you maintain exposure and prevent camera shake.
- **Make Gorgeous Bokeh:** You may create beautiful, smooth bokeh that makes your subject stand out even more by using a wide aperture, such as f/1.7. The out-of-focus areas in your picture are called bokeh. The dreamy, gentle appearance of the fuzzy background highlights your subject and minimizes the visibility of any distracting objects behind them. **Pro Tip:** Try taking pictures with candles, street lights, or any other strong background light sources to achieve the best bokeh. Observe how the lights transform into rounded, smooth forms. The number of aperture blades in your lens will also affect

the shape of the bokeh. More curved blades will give the result a more appealing and natural appearance.

- **Pay Attention to Accuracy:** Focus can be easily lost due to the small depth of field at f/1.7, particularly when working with fast-moving subjects or while autofocus is engaged. The focus plane is so tiny that you have to be quite accurate. Make sure the topic is very clear by paying great attention to your focus points and taking your time if you're shooting manually. **Pro Tip:** Make use of single point autofocus if your camera has it. Use manual focus if you want to be certain that you have exact control. It's also a good idea to use your camera's depth of field preview button to see how much of your image will be in focus at f/1.7.

- **Flare Control Lens:** Wide apertures like f/1.7 can sometimes result in lens flare if you're shooting directly into bright light sources like the sun or artificial lights. While flare can occasionally provide a lovely artistic touch, it can also reduce contrast and clarity in images. **Pro Tip:** Try shooting from different angles or use a lens hood to block out unwanted light to regulate the amount of flare that enters the lens ring. Even if you don't want that look, avoiding intense direct light will help you maintain a crisp and clean image.

- **Try out Different Creative Effects:** F/1.7 has several advantages, including the ability to capture clear, sharp features. Additionally, it's an aperture that can assist you in creating art that has a really distinct appearance. Whether you're focusing on minute details like flowers or textures or shooting wide open for a dreamlike effect, this portrait aperture lets you play around with the way the subject and background interact. Use the "focus and recompose" technique as a pro tip. Concentrate on a single aspect of your subject, and then alter the composition while maintaining your attention on it. Depending on your viewpoint, the blurry background can change, allowing you to see things creatively.

CHAPTER SIX
SHOOTING AND AUTOFOCUS MODES
An explanation of phase detection autofocus (PDAF)

Cameras that use Phase Detection Autofocus (PDAF) technology have faster and more accurate autofocus. It differs from conventional contrast-detection autofocus, which uses back-and-forth lens adjustments to find the sharpest image. More sophisticated and professional cameras, such as the Leica Q3 43, frequently employ PDAF since it is faster and more dependable than contrast detection, which can be slow. PDAF, to put it simply, uses a unique sensor to "measure" the phase difference between light comings into the camera from two different locations. With this method, the sensor is divided into a grid, and tiny photodiodes are positioned at various points. The light from these several locations is compared by the camera. The camera recognizes that the lens needs to be adjusted when the light waves are out of phase. The camera detects that the image is in focus when the light waves are precisely in phase or synchronized. Speed is PDAF's best feature. It enables the camera to focus significantly faster than with conventional techniques, which makes it great for subjects that move quickly or for situations when you don't want to wait for the camera to "hunt" for focus. Professional photographers adore PDAF in part because of this. It's particularly helpful in fast-paced environments, such as wildlife or sports photography.

Focusing on a subject is remarkably quick and accurate with the Leica Q3 43, which probably employs some kind of PDAF. The camera maintains sharpness when monitoring a moving subject by adjusting focus very quickly. You may concentrate more on planning your shot rather than worrying about the technical details because the technology handles a lot of the labor-intensive work. The drawback of PDAF is that it requires certain sensors to function properly; therefore the camera must have the right autofocus system and sensor array. Thankfully, the Leica Q3 43 was created with this in mind, guaranteeing that PDAF functions flawlessly in the majority of circumstances. To put it briefly, one of the factors that allows contemporary cameras, like the Leica Q3 43, to focus so rapidly and precisely is Phase Detection Autofocus (PDAF). It's revolutionary for photographers who want quick, accurate focus, particularly when working with moving subjects or hectic settings.

Focus Peaking and Manual Focus

Although they are commonly disregarded in the era of autofocus, manual focus and focus peaking are two capabilities of contemporary cameras that are immensely effective for individuals who desire greater control over their photos. Photographers who wish to adjust their focus instead of depending entirely on the camera's autofocus function will find these capabilities especially helpful. Let's dissect them:

Manual Focus (MF)

The term "manual focus," which is frequently shortened to "MF," refers to the fact that the photographer is responsible for focusing the camera. To bring the subject into sharp focus, you spin the lens's focus ring rather than relying on the camera to select the focus point. This gives you total control over your attention, which is helpful in many circumstances. For instance, manual focus enables you to accurately adjust the focus on the little subject you're photographing in macro photography, when the depth of field is incredibly thin. Similar to this, the camera's autofocus may not work well in low light or low contrast situations, but you can make sure your subject is as sharp as you want it to be by using manual focus. The manual focus feature of the Leica Q3 43 allows you to change the focus without relying on the camera to "guess" what you want in focus. To shift the focus point, adjust the focus ring on the lens. Even though manual focus might occasionally be slower than autofocus, the amount of control it provides can make up for it, particularly in highly controlled or artistic shooting scenarios.

Peaking Focus

Now, manual focus can be a little challenging, particularly when you're attempting to focus on a small object in a macro image or a person's eye in a portrait. Focus peaking is useful in this situation. A technique called focus peaking draws attention to the parts of the picture that are in focus. To make it easy to discern where the focus is greatest, these regions are frequently delineated with a vivid hue (such as red, yellow, or green). It serves as a kind of visual aid that indicates precisely which areas of the frame are in focus. For instance, if you're taking a portrait with the Leica Q3 43 in manual focus mode, you might want to focus specifically on the subject's eye. The sharpest portion of the image will light up brightly as you adjust the focus, letting you know that you have the proper area in focus. This greatly simplifies manual focusing, particularly in difficult situations where it's difficult to identify what's in focus simply by looking at the screen, or while dealing with a shallow depth of field. When shooting in video mode, where you frequently need to maintain a subject's focus while they move or while you adjust your composition, focus peaking is really helpful. You probably have a peaking option with the Q3 43, which will help you keep everything precisely where you want it, without having to guess.

How Everything Comes Together

You get the best of both worlds when you combine focus peaking with manual focus. You may manually adjust the focus to the precise level you choose, and focus peaking allows you to see if you're on point. Without depending on autofocus to make choices for you, it's a fantastic method to make sure you're focusing where you wish to.

When to Employ Focus Peaking and Manual Focus

- **Low-Light Conditions:** When there is minimal contrast in the scene or in low light, autofocus may have trouble. Focus peaking in conjunction with manual focus gives you the confidence to concentrate even in challenging lighting situations.
- **Creative Control:** You may wish to manually adjust what is in focus in certain creative creations. For instance, manual focus enables you to precisely highlight a certain area of the picture, such as the eye of the subject or a detail in a landscape.
- **Fast-moving Subjects:** Autofocus is capable of tracking subjects, but it occasionally struggles to keep up with intricate sceneries or rapid motion. Manual focus can help you make sure you don't miss the shot if you want complete control over what's in focus.
- **Macro Photography:** Because of the extremely shallow depth of field in macro photography, you have more control over even the smallest details when you use manual focus.

With the help of strong capabilities like manual focus and focus peaking, you can fully manage your focus and receive precise, detailed results. These tools are essential for a camera like the Leica Q3 43, which is made for professionals and enthusiasts who value accuracy and fine details. Even if you're not utilizing autofocus, manual focus combined with focus peaking makes the process simpler and more dependable, whether you're shooting in low light, trying to capture minute details, or simply want to make sure your focus is precise. It all comes down to allowing you the flexibility to produce the pictures you want.

Face and Eye Detection Capabilities

Characteristics like face and eye detection have grown in importance in contemporary cameras, particularly for portraiture and other scenarios where it's critical to capture a subject's facial characteristics in fine focus. These features, which frequently beat manual focus in terms of speed and accuracy, use artificial intelligence (AI) or specialized algorithms to automatically recognize and concentrate on a subject's face and eyes. Let's examine the operation and performance of face and eye identification, specifically in the Leica Q3 43.

Face and Eye Detection: What Is It?

A technique called face detection recognizes people's faces in photos automatically. When activated, the autofocus feature of your camera will focus on a face instead of the background or other objects in the frame. When there are several topics in a picture and you want to make sure the face is the main focus, it's quite useful. By identifying and focusing on a subject's eyes, which are frequently the most important aspect of a portrait, eye detection goes one step further. Because eyes are typically the main focus of portrait photography, having them sharp and in focus is frequently what makes or breaks the shot, so this is really helpful.

How It Operates

By using the camera's autofocus technology to analyze the image and identify the patterns and characteristics indicative of a human face, face and eye detection operates. Even in intricate scenes, the camera's software then separates these regions and modifies the focus appropriately. These technologies are included into the Leica Q3 43's sophisticated autofocus systems, which enable it to discern faces and eyes with speed and accuracy. **The system normally operates as follows:**

- **Face Detection:** The camera looks for faces in the image. As soon as it recognizes a face, it gives that region top priority and makes sure it is sharp.
- **Eye Detection:** Even if the subject is moving, the camera will focus on the eyes and perform additional facial analysis if it detects that a face is in the picture. This guarantees that the eyes are always sharply focused, which is crucial for taking portraits.

Many cameras use artificial intelligence (AI) algorithms to distinguish faces from other objects in the picture by searching for facial features like the mouth, nose, and eyes. The camera will automatically follow the face or eye once it has been detected, focusing as the subject moves.

Leica Q3 43 Face and Eye Detection

You can anticipate remarkable face and eye detection performance from the Leica Q3 43, which is renowned for its accuracy and cutting-edge technology. Leica often incorporates top-notch autofocus systems with complex face and eye detection algorithms. **What to anticipate is as follows:**

- **Speed and Accuracy:** Even if a face is moving within the picture, the camera can detect and focus on it rapidly. The camera is extremely quick for portraiture or scenarios where you need to capture expressions in a split second because it will lock focus on a face practically instantly as it is recognized.
- **Eye Detection:** Essential for portrait photography, the Leica Q3 43 can identify and focus on a subject's eyes in addition to faces. As a result, you won't need to manually adjust the focus to get clear, sharp images—the camera will take care of that. Sharp eyes are generally the focal point of portraits, therefore possessing this quality is very beneficial.
- **Tracking Moving Subjects:** The capacity of face and eye detection to maintain focus on moving objects is one of its most notable features. Even in dynamic scenarios, such as when a person is strolling or dancing, the camera may follow the subject's face (or eyes) as they move across the frame. Because of this, it can be used for more dynamic, real-life photography in addition to posed pictures.
- **Lighting Conditions:** The Leica Q3 43's and other contemporary face and eye identification systems are made to function well in a range of lighting situations. The system can swiftly and reliably detect faces and eyes in most typical lighting settings, while it may still have some trouble in challenging low light. To make sure the subject looks their best, the camera will make every effort to focus on the face and eyes, even in backlit situations.

Making Use of the Various Shooting Modes

A world of creative possibilities can be unlocked by learning and utilizing your camera's many shooting modes. Every mode has a distinct function and can assist you in taking pictures in a range of settings, from quick action shots to exquisitely arranged landscapes or portraits. Let's examine some of the typical shooting modes found on cameras like as the Leica Q3 43 and discuss how to make the most of them.

Auto Mode

The easiest setting to use on any camera is auto mode. Most of the decisions, including focus, ISO, shutter speed, and aperture, are made by the camera when you switch to Auto. It works well when you want to capture a good picture but don't want to spend time changing settings. Auto mode is practical, but it doesn't let you be very creative. The camera's algorithms make all the decisions for you, which occasionally lead to less-than-ideal results. For instance, Auto mode might not always choose the ideal exposure or might have trouble in dimly lit environments. Having said that, it's a fantastic place to start for novices or for situations where you need to take a fast picture.

The Program Mode (P)

Auto is not as good as Program Mode. Although the camera chooses the exposure parameters (aperture and shutter speed) automatically in this mode, you still have more control because you can change other parameters like ISO and white balance. Program Mode is ideal if you want to maintain automatic exposure while having a little more creative freedom. Although the camera adjusts the shutter speed and aperture according to the lighting, you can change those settings by using the control dial to choose between various shutter speed and aperture combinations (also called Program Shift). This allows you to play around with different looks a bit more without going into full manual settings.

Aperture Priority Mode (A or Av)

Photographers who wish to manage the depth of field—the amount of the image that is in focus—while letting the camera determine the shutter speed prefer to use the Aperture Priority setting. In this mode, the camera will automatically determine the shutter speed to maintain the correct exposure while you manually choose the aperture (f-stop). When you wish to isolate your subject with a blurry background (by using a wide aperture, such as f/1.8) or when shooting in different lighting circumstances, this setting is great. While allowing the camera to manage the technical aspects of shutter speed, it allows you to control the artistic component of the image, such as how much or how little is in focus.

Shutter Priority Mode (TV or S)

If you want to manage the way motion is caught in your pictures, Shutter Priority mode is perfect. When you choose the shutter speed in this mode, the camera modifies the aperture to achieve the right exposure. It works well for subjects that move quickly, as well as for creating motion blur or freezing motion. For instance, you would use a rapid shutter speed (such as 1/1000 or quicker) to stop the motion when taking pictures of a moving subject, such as an automobile or runner. You might use a slower shutter speed (such as 1/4 or 1/2 second) if you were photographing a waterfall and wanted to get a gentle, dreamy blur of the water flowing. You can concentrate on motion control in Shutter Priority mode rather than bothering about aperture adjustments.

The Manual Mode (M)

Photographers who desire total control over every setting should use the Manual Mode. To achieve the precise exposure you want, you manually modify the shutter speed, aperture, and ISO in this mode. You can really adjust every element of your shot in this mode to fit your artistic vision. The ideal choice for people who want complete control over their exposure, particularly in difficult lighting situations, is Manual Mode, despite the fact that it may initially seem daunting. Manual Mode lets you tweak every detail to make sure the picture is just the way you want it, whether you're photographing a sunset or a portrait in a poorly lit space. For individuals who have mastered exposure fundamentals and wish to go further into the technical aspects of photography, this mode is ideal.

Burst Mode (Continuous/Continuous Shooting Mode)

As long as you keep the shutter button depressed, the camera will snap several quick shots in burst or continuous shooting mode. For action photographs, sports photography, or any scenario where the subject is moving swiftly, this setting is ideal. By providing you with a selection of pictures, it guarantees that you won't miss the ideal opportunity. Burst mode, for instance, enables you to take numerous pictures in a short period of time, such as when you're photographing a child playing soccer or an animal rushing. The Leica Q3 43's burst mode increases your chances of getting the ideal photo and is quick enough to catch subjects that move quickly.

Mode of Portrait

Portrait mode is a preset setting created especially for taking attractive, well-lit pictures of people. The subject will be sharply focused and the backdrop will be blurred as the camera automatically adjusts the aperture to produce a shallow depth of field. Whether you're using a zoom lens or a prime lens like the 35mm, this is ideal for taking portraits. Additionally, portrait mode frequently adjusts exposure and color balance to accentuate skin tones, making your subject appear more attractive and natural. Portrait Mode takes care of everything for you if you're taking a quick portrait and want to ensure that the subject's face is sharp while the surrounding is soft and out of focus.

Using Landscape Mode

By optimizing depth of field, landscape mode makes sure that every element in the picture, from the background to the foreground, is sharp. To do this, the camera usually uses a smaller aperture (higher f-stop). When photographing cityscapes, expansive panoramas, or any other scenario where you want the entire image to be in focus, this is perfect. The camera may also change the color balance in this mode to enhance the vibrancy of the blues and greens, highlighting the beauty of the natural world. Landscape Mode will assist guarantee that your images have the most clarity possible throughout the picture if you're photographing expansive areas, such as a shoreline or a mountain range.

Portrait Mode at Night

The purpose of the Night Portrait mode is to take pictures of people in low light, such as at night or at dusk. To let as much light into the lens as possible, the camera will automatically utilize a larger aperture and a slower shutter speed. Additionally, it can set off the flash to capture the background ambient light while illuminating the foreground subject. When you want to take a nighttime picture of someone with a striking background, this is a terrific mode to utilize. While preserving the beauty of the nighttime scene, the camera's settings will guarantee that the subject is appropriately exposed.

Scene Modes: Sports, Close-up, Scenic, etc.

A number of specialist scene modes are available on several cameras, such as the Leica Q3 43, to optimize settings for particular kinds of shooting.
Among these modes are:
- Macro Mode (Close-Up Mode): Used to capture tiny objects, such as insects or flowers.
- **Sports Mode**: This setting allows the camera to choose quicker shutter speeds for subjects that move quickly, such as athletes or animals.
- Panorama Mode: This feature assists you in capturing expansive, sweeping vistas by directing you through the process of taking several pictures, which the camera will then combine into a panoramic picture.

Without requiring manual setting adjustments, these scene modes are made to make it simple for photographers to get excellent results in particular situations. Your Leica Q3 43's multiple shooting modes are tools to help you get the finest shots in diverse scenarios. Whether you want to photograph portraits with flawless bokeh, record quick motion, or have more control over your exposure, each mode is made with a specific goal in mind. You may advance your photography and produce pictures that accurately convey your artistic vision by being aware of how each mode functions and when to apply it.

CHAPTER SEVEN
MASTERING EXPOSURE AND METERING
Comprehending ISO, Aperture, and Shutter Speed

Gaining proficiency in photography requires an understanding of ISO, shutter speed, and aperture. These three settings are the foundation of exposure, and each one affects the final quality of your picture in a different way. When combined, they create what photographers call the "exposure triangle." Let's dissect them in a straightforward and useful manner, particularly when utilizing a camera such as the Leica Q3 43.

ISO: The Light Sensitivity

The ISO regulates how sensitive the camera sensor is to light. Put more simply, it uses the available light to determine how bright or dark your image will be.
- Low ISO (such as ISO 100 or 200): Because the camera is less sensitive to light while using a low ISO, a dark image will result from insufficient light. However, a low ISO has the advantage of maintaining a clear, sharp image with little noise or grain. Low ISO works well in bright settings, such as a sunny day outside.
- High ISO (such as ISO 1600 or 3200): This makes it easier to take pictures in low light by increasing the sensor's sensitivity to light. But raising the ISO also causes grain or noise to appear in the picture. The quality of your photo may suffer as the ISO increases since noise becomes more apparent. However, a higher ISO enables you to obtain a properly exposed image in scenarios where you need to swiftly capture a subject, such as inside or at night.

When ISO should be changed

- To preserve image quality in well-lit environments, use a low ISO.
- If you require higher shutter speeds or are shooting in low light, raise the ISO to prevent motion blur, but be careful not to add too much noise.

Shutter Speed: Exposure Duration

The length of time the camera's sensor is exposed to light is controlled by the shutter speed. Seconds or fractions of a second (such as 1/500, 1/60, or 1/2) are used to measure it. Light strikes the sensor less frequently at faster shutter speeds and more frequently at slower shutter speeds.
- **Fast Shutter Speed (such as 1/1000 or 1/500):** Light enters a camera at a fast shutter speed for a brief period of time. This works well for freezing subjects that move quickly, such as a speeding car, a runner, or a bird in flight. It guarantees that quick movements are recorded in a clear and sharp manner and helps avoid motion blur. The drawback is

that, in low light, there may not be enough time for the sensor to gather enough light, which could lead to underexposed photos.

- **Slow Shutter Speed:** A slow shutter speed allows light to enter the camera for a longer amount of time. Examples of this include 1/30, 1/4, or even multiple seconds. This is perfect for producing creative effects like light trails or blurred motion in flowing water, or for capturing more light in low-light situations (such as photographing at night). However, if the subject is moving or the camera isn't steady, a lower shutter speed can also cause motion blur.

When to change the shutter speed

- When shooting in bright light or needing to freeze motion, use a quick shutter speed.
- For artistic effects like motion blur or to capture more light in poor light, use a slow shutter speed.

Aperture: The Dimensions of the Lens's Opening

The amount of light that enters the camera through the lens is controlled by aperture. F-stops (such as f/1.8, f/5.6, and f/16) are used to quantify it. **The depth of field, or how much of the image is in focus from the foreground to the background, is also influenced by the aperture.**

- **Wide Aperture (e.g., f/1.4, f/2.8):** A wide aperture signifies a bigger opening, which allows more light to hit the sensor. This is perfect for low-light circumstances or when you want to produce a shallow depth of field. A shallow depth of field results in a fuzzy background, helping your subject stands out sharply against a soft backdrop. Wide apertures are frequently used in portraiture to get this effect, which puts the subject's face in focus and the backdrop artfully blurred.
- **Narrow Aperture:** A narrow aperture, such as f/8 or f/16, results in a narrower opening, which lets less light into the sensor. A narrower aperture, on the other hand, results in a greater depth of field, which means that more of the image will be in focus from front to back. When photographing architecture or landscapes, where you want everything to be crisp and clear, this is helpful.

When to change the aperture

- When you need to capture more light in low light or when you want a shallow depth of field, choose a wide aperture (low f-stop number).
- If you want a deeper focus or wish to avoid overexposure when shooting in bright light, use a narrow aperture (higher f-stop number).

The Exposure Triangle: The Interaction of these Environments

Together, the ISO, shutter speed, and aperture settings determine exposure, or how light or dark your picture is.

You must strike a balance based on the circumstances because changing one will have an impact on the others.

- To get a brighter picture, widen the aperture, lower the shutter speed, or raise the ISO.
- To achieve a darker image, narrow the aperture, increase the shutter speed, or lower the ISO.

Case 1: Low-Light Situation If you're shooting at night or in a poorly light space, you could:

- To increase the sensor's sensitivity to light, raise the ISO.
- To let in more light, open the aperture (choose a smaller f-number).
- To gradually capture enough light, reduce the shutter speed.

But exercise caution! Your image may appear grainy if you increase the ISO too much. Motion blur may result from a shutter speed that is too slow, particularly if you are not using a tripod.

Case 2: Action Photography When shooting a subject that moves quickly, such as a soccer player or a bird in flight, you would probably:

- To stop motion, use a fast shutter speed.
- Because rapid shutter speeds let in less light, open the aperture (choose a smaller f-number) to capture as much light as you can.
- To prevent noise, strive to keep the ISO as low as possible while adjusting it appropriately.

Useful Advice for the Leica Q3 43

- In daylight: To guarantee sharpness and prevent overexposure, you may frequently get away with using a low ISO (100–400), a quick shutter speed (1/1000 or 1/500), and a narrower aperture (f/8 to f/16).
- In low light, you may need to use a wider aperture (f/2.8), slow down the shutter speed (e.g., 1/30 or slower), and increase the ISO (e.g., 800-1600) in order to let in more light. Just be careful not to introduce motion blur with slow shutter speeds or noise with higher ISO.

When to Use Different Metering Modes

By measuring the amount of light in a scene, metering modes—a crucial component of a camera—assist in determining the proper exposure. Using sensors to measure light, the camera's metering system determines the ideal shutter speed, aperture, and ISO to make sure the picture is neither too dark (underexposed) nor too bright (overexposed). The majority of contemporary cameras, like the Leica Q3 43, have multiple metering settings, each of which operates differently. Your ability to take well-exposed photos in a range of scenarios can be greatly enhanced by knowing when and how to use each metering mode. Let's review the primary metering modes and their potential applications.

Metric/Evaluative Metering

How it operates: The most popular metering mode in contemporary cameras is Evaluative or Matrix Metering. To determine the ideal exposure, it separates the scene into several zones and assesses the light in each. To determine the ideal overall exposure, the camera makes use of its sensor and its understanding of common settings, such as brilliant skies or dark shadows. This mode is intended to provide you with a balanced exposure and performs effectively in the majority of circumstances.

When to apply it

+ **General Use:** When you're taking pictures of scenes with a range of light and shadow or when you're unsure about the lighting in your scene, this is an excellent all-around setting.
+ **Landscape Photography:** Matrix metering will try its best to adjust the exposure so you don't lose detail in any area when the image has both dark (like mountains) and bright (like the sky).
+ **Street Photography:** Evaluative metering automatically modifies the exposure for the best photo in erratic lighting conditions, such as on a street with a mix of highlights and shadows.

Use it because it provides a consistent exposure without requiring you to manually adjust for different light levels. To prevent underexposing or overexposing specific parts, the camera's algorithm takes the entire picture into account.

Weighed Center Metering

How it works: Center-weighted metering prioritizes the central region of the frame while measuring light throughout the scene. The exposure of the central region is given a lot of weight, yet the overall scene's light is averaged. Regardless of the rest of the picture, this is helpful when the subject is in the middle of the frame and you want to make sure they are properly exposed.

When to apply it

+ **Portrait Photography:** Regardless of how much lighter or darker the background is, you want to make sure that your subject's face is properly illuminated while they are in the center of the frame.
+ **Clear Focal Point Situations:** These are those in which you want a subject or object in the center of the picture to be well exposed (e.g., a crucial object in a busy scene or a single person in a landscape).
+ **Backlit Scenes:** Even if the background is significantly brighter, the camera can still prioritize exposing the subject if it is backlit, such as in front of the sun or a bright window.
+ **Why use it:** When your subject is the focal point of the composition and you wish to concentrate the exposure on that region, this metering mode is perfect. This is especially true when the subject is surrounded by sizable regions of strong light or darkness.

Spot Metering

How it operates: Spot metering measures light in a very small, precise region of the frame, usually in the middle, though some cameras let you adjust the spot to other areas. You can meter off a tiny portion of the scene, such as a person's face or a particular detail, using this mode, which offers you exact control over the exposure. This small area serves as the basis for calculating exposure; the remainder of the scene is disregarded.

When to apply it

- **High Contrast Scenes:** Spot metering helps you expose the subject so they don't appear too dark (underexposed) or too bright (overexposed) while you're photographing them in front of a strong light source or against a very dark background.
- **Photographs in Strong Lighting:** Spot metering can guarantee that the subject's face is appropriately lit when taking photographs, particularly in strong light or in a studio setting.
- **Highlight or Shadow Detail:** Regardless of what else is happening in the image, spot metering will guarantee that you can expose that precise area accurately if you want to capture a particular detail, such the highlights on an object or the shadow of a subject.
- **Why use it:** For accuracy, spot metering is excellent. Spot metering allows you to manage the exposure of a small portion of your composition, such as a subject or a person's face, even if the surrounding portions are extremely light or dark.

Partial metering

How it operates: Although partial metering covers a wider region of the frame, it functions similarly to spot metering. It usually occupies ten to fifteen percent of the image's center. It offers greater flexibility while maintaining focus on the focal point of the scene, serving as a compromise between center-weighted and spot metering.

When to apply it

- **When You Want More Area than Spot Metering:** Partial metering is helpful if you want to meter across an area that is somewhat larger than a tiny spot but still want the center to be the focus.
- **Backlighting or Strong Contrast:** Partial metering can appropriately expose the center of the frame in scenes with high contrast without making the backdrop overpowering the exposure computations.
- **Why use it:** When the topic is significant but has a little more background than spot metering would offer partial metering works best. By taking into account a wider surrounding environment, it helps you acquire a balanced exposure to the issue.

Highlight-Weighted Metering (certain cameras have this feature)

How it works: To prevent overexposure in bright regions, highlight-weighted metering is intended to give priority to the highlights in a scene. In order to maintain detail in the brightest areas of the picture, like a bright sky, polished surfaces, or light-colored objects, the camera will modify exposure.

When to apply it

- **Scenes with Bright Highlights:** This metering mode helps prevent the brightest parts from losing clarity and being overexposed if you're shooting in an environment with bright highlights, such as a landscape at sunrise or sunset or a scene with a lot of reflective surfaces.
- **Shooting Snow or Water:** The brilliant, shiny surfaces of snowy landscapes and bodies of water can quickly become overexposed when photographed. This is controlled by highlight-weighted metering, which makes sure certain regions maintain detail.
- **Why use it:** When highlight detail is important and you don't want to lose bright regions in your photos, this metering setting is perfect.

A Real-World Example Using the Leica Q3 43

Assume that a bright sky is in the background of a portrait you are taking. In this instance:

- The subject may be underexposed since the camera also aims to expose the bright sky, even while evaluation metering may try to balance exposure for the subject and the sky.
- Spot Metering might be a preferable option in this case since it would ignore the bright sky and concentrate on the subject's face, which is the most crucial area to make sure they are exposed appropriately.
- If the subject is positioned in the middle of the frame, center-weighted metering may be helpful in making sure they are adequately exposed while taking the background into account.

The lighting conditions, your subject, and the elements you wish to highlight in your shot all influence the metering mode you choose. Spot or Center-Weighted Metering can be quite helpful when you need control or precision over the exposure of particular parts in the frame, even though Evaluative/Matrix Metering is the most flexible and generally effective. You can make the most of your camera's features, like those on the Leica Q3 43, to get more imaginative and accurate exposures if you know when to utilize each mode.

Compensation for Exposure and Bracketing

Two crucial photography techniques that provide you more control over exposure are exposure compensation and bracketing. These tools let you modify the final image to fit your creative vision or make sure you obtain the ideal shot in challenging lighting situations. Both are helpful if you wish to adjust the exposure slightly to achieve the desired effect while working with automatic settings.

Adapting Exposure to Your Requirements through Exposure Compensation

- **What it is:** With exposure compensation, you can change the exposure (brightness or darkness) of your picture while still utilizing the camera's automatic or semi-automatic settings (such as Program Mode, Shutter Priority, or Aperture Priority). In challenging lighting situations, such as high contrast scenes, backlighting, or situations with a combination of bright and dark parts, the camera's exposure calculation based on its metering may not always be accurate. You can instruct the camera to lighten or darken the image by a certain amount by utilizing exposure compensation. Stops (e.g., +1, -2), which indicate doubling or halving the quantity of light in the image, are used to assess this correction. For instance, you can increase the exposure by one stop if it's too dark and lower it by one stop if it's too light.

- **How to utilize it:** Usually, you press a button or turn a dial on your camera to activate exposure correction. For instance, you may change the exposure setting on the Leica Q3 43 by using the exposure compensation slider. Images with positive values (+) are brighter, while those with negative values (-) are darker.

When exposure compensation should be used

- **Backlit subjects:** The camera may expose the bright background, making the subject overly dark, if you're taking pictures of someone or something in front of a bright background, such as the sky or a window. Exposure compensation can be used to brighten your subject and boost exposure.
- **High contrast scenes:** Exposure compensation helps you make sure you don't miss any crucial details in the highlights or shadows when you're photographing a picture that has both brilliant highlights and dark shadows, such as a nighttime metropolis or a sunset.
- **Snow or reflective surfaces:** Reflective surfaces, such as snow or water, can cause the camera's metering mechanism to underexpose the picture. You can obtain a more realistic depiction of the brightness of the scene by raising the exposure by one or two stops.

For instance: When photographing someone against a bright sky, the camera may expose the sky, making the subject's face appear too dark. The camera can brighten the image and make the subject's face more visible without totally overexposing the sky by setting the exposure correction to +1 or +2.

Why make use of it: You can use automatic settings with greater flexibility thanks to exposure compensation. To adjust the exposure, you don't need to bother about switching to full manual mode. It's a fast, simple method to instantly change the image's brightness or darkness, guaranteeing that you acquire the precise exposure you require with minimal work.

The practice of taking many exposures, or exposure bracketing

- **What it is:** Using the exposure bracketing approach, the camera captures multiple images of the same scene at various exposure levels. Usually, three or more photographs are taken in succession: one at the suggested exposure for the camera, one underexposed, and one overexposed. Bracketing is a technique used to make sure you get the best exposure, particularly in difficult lighting conditions where you're not sure if the settings you've picked will work. You will usually get images with exposure values of -1, 0, and +1 stops, which means one shot will be underexposed, one will be correctly exposed, and one will be overexposed. However, the range of exposure adjustments can vary. This provides you with a collection of pictures from which to select the best one. The images can also be utilized for HDR (High Dynamic Range) photography, which combines several exposures to produce a single picture that captures a wider variety of highlights and shadows.

+ **How to utilize it:** Exposure bracketing is often activated by a dedicated dial or in the menu of your camera. You may configure exposure bracketing on the Leica Q3 43 by selecting an option in the shooting menu. The number of photos you wish to take and the exposure range between them (e.g., 1 stop or 2 stops) are up to you. Once bracketing is enabled, when you push the shutter, the camera will automatically capture a series of bracketed images with varying exposure values. Between pictures, you won't have to manually change the settings.

When exposure bracketing should be used

+ **High Dynamic Range (HDR) photography:** By using bracketing, you can make sure you catch every detail in a subject with a broad range of brightness, such as a sunset or a brightly lit room with deep shadows. You can then combine the information to create an HDR image that looks more realistic.

+ **Tough lighting conditions:** Bracketing enables you to take many pictures and select the one with the optimal exposure if you're not sure if the camera's metering will provide you with the correct exposure (such as a subject with both bright highlights and dark shadows).

+ **Landscape photography:** Bracketing helps you acquire the ideal exposure while taking pictures of high contrast landscapes, like those taken at golden hour or twilight, so you can capture the nuances in the highlights and shadows.

For instance: Consider taking pictures of a city at dusk. Despite the sky's extreme brightness, the foreground buildings are considerably darker. Your camera will take three pictures when you use exposure bracketing: one with the sky properly exposed, one with the buildings underexposed, and one with the shadows overexposed to bring out more detail. For a more balanced HDR image, you can subsequently blend them or select the optimal exposure.

Why make use of it: When the light is difficult and you want to be sure you're getting the greatest exposure possible, exposure bracketing is a huge help. Additionally, it provides you with a collection of photographs from which you may select the finest one or combine them to create a high-quality HDR image.

Important distinctions between bracketing and exposure compensation

+ Adjusting the exposure for a single photo is known as exposure compensation. You adjust the exposure by dialing in the desired amount, and the camera will make the necessary adjustments. It is quick, simple to use, and effective in circumstances where you are uncertain about the exposure.

- **Exposure bracketing:** This technique is capturing many pictures at various exposures, providing you with a variety of choices that you may later combine. Bracketing is very helpful when creating HDR photographs or in situations with a lot of contrast.

For achieving the ideal exposure in your photographs, Exposure Bracketing and Exposure Compensation are both effective techniques. When you need to quickly fine-tune the exposure, exposure compensation is ideal because it lets you change the brightness of a single image on the fly. However, while working with difficult lighting, exposure bracketing ensures that you get the greatest exposure possible by providing you with a range of exposures. On a camera like the Leica Q3 43, both capabilities are immensely useful since they provide you flexibility and control when it comes to producing detailed, well-exposed photos.

Making Use of the Integrated ND Filter

Many high-end cameras, like as the Leica Q3 43 model, have a useful built-in ND (Neutral Density) filter that lets users adjust the amount of light that enters the lens without changing the color balance. It's particularly helpful when you wish to use slower shutter speeds or wider apertures than would be feasible in bright light. To maximize your photos, let's examine what a built-in ND filter does, how it operates, and when to use it.

Neutral Density (ND) Filters: What Are They?

In essence, an ND filter is a piece of optical glass or resin that lowers the quantity of light entering the lens without changing the scene's color. Similar to sunglasses for your camera, the filter lessens the amount of light that reaches the sensor while maintaining the same appearance. **There are several strengths of ND filters; more light reduction is indicated by higher numbers.**

- A built-in ND filter eliminates the need to screw on or affix a separate filter to your lens because it is integrated within the camera body. For photographers who wish to employ ND filtering without requiring additional equipment, this makes it quite convenient.
-

How Do Integrated ND Filters Operate?

You may modify your settings without overexposing your photo thanks to the built-in ND filter, which reduces the amount of light that enters the camera. For instance, if you want to use a wide aperture (such as f/1.8) to get a shallow depth of focus while shooting outside on a bright, sunny day, the image can be overexposed due to too much light entering the lens. The camera lowers the amount of light entering by turning on the ND filter, which lets you keep the aperture open without overexposing the picture. Usually, the built-in ND filter has a predetermined density, like a 3-stop or 4-stop light reduction. In strong lighting, you can use wider apertures or longer shutter speeds because it reduces the amount of light by three or four stops.

When to Apply an Integrated ND Filter

In the following situations, an integrated ND filter can be especially helpful:

- **Taking Pictures in Bright Light:** The ND filter can assist in lowering the total amount of light entering the camera while you're shooting in bright environments, like midday on a sunny day. **This prevents your image from being overexposed when you utilize slower shutter speeds or larger apertures. For instance:**
  - ➢ Wide Aperture for Shallow Depth of Field: To achieve a blurry backdrop, you should use a wide aperture (such as f/1.8 or f/2.8), but the intense sunshine overexposes the picture. You can use the wide aperture without worrying about overexposure by turning on the ND filter, which will blur the backdrop while maintaining focus on your subject.

- **Photography with Extended Exposure:** Slower shutter speeds are necessary for long exposure photographs, such those that capture the action of flowing water, nighttime traffic, or a smooth sky. However, a slow shutter speed could result in overexposure in bright light. By lowering the quantity of light entering the camera, an ND filter lets you use a longer exposure without overexposing the picture. An ND filter, for instance, enables you to slow down the shutter speed to get the smooth, flowing water appearance without over-brightening the picture if you wish to photograph the motion of waves on a beach during the day.

- **Recording Videos:** Maintaining a natural-looking motion blur during video recording is crucial, and this is usually accomplished by employing a shutter speed double the frame rate (e.g., 1/50 for 24fps video). However, this setting could lead to an overexposed video if you're shooting in direct sunlight. By avoiding overexposure, the ND filter enables you to maintain your shutter speed within the intended range.

- **Managing Exposure in Scenes with High Contrast:** When photographing scenes that have both dark shadows and dazzling highlights, you might wish to appropriately expose the shadows without blowing out the highlights. By lowering the amount of light entering the camera, the ND filter can help balance exposure without changing the scene's overall color balance.

- **Managing Motion Blur:** You may use a slow shutter speed to purposefully blur the movement of your subjects if you're photographing them moving quickly. By lowering the amount of light that enters the camera, the ND filter can enable you use a slower shutter speed in strong lighting without overexposing the picture.

Real-World Example: Making Use of the Leica Q3 43's Built-In ND Filter

Consider using the Leica Q3 43 to take a portrait outside in direct sunshine. When you choose a wide aperture, such as f/1.8, you want to obtain a small depth of field; however, the result is an overexposed photograph. You may maintain the aperture wide while avoiding overexposure by using the built-in ND filter, which lowers the amount of light entering the camera, rather than changing the shutter speed or ISO. Similar to this, if you're photographing a waterfall in the daylight and want to use a slow shutter speed (let's say 1/4 or 1/2 second) to achieve a smooth, silky motion impression, the ND filter will help you do so without allowing the image to become overexposed from the intense external illumination.

Benefits of an Integrated ND Filter

- **Convenience:** You don't need to carry along additional ND filters that you have to screw on and off the lens because the ND filter is built into the camera. When necessary, you may easily turn the ND filter on or off.
- **Space-saving:** You won't have to bring along extra equipment, which is particularly useful if you like a simple setup or want to keep your equipment as light as possible.
- **Consistency:** Unlike third-party filters, which can occasionally introduce undesired color shifts or distortions, built-in ND filters are usually made to work in unison with the camera's exposure system.

Drawbacks

- **Fixed Strength:** Typically, an integrated ND filter has a set amount of light attenuation (e.g., 3 stops or 4 stops). You would have to use an external ND filter if you require a greater or lesser amount of light reduction.
- **Restricted to Specific Shooting Modes:** The built-in ND filter may only function in specific modes or with particular lens settings, depending on your camera's settings. It's a good idea to consult your camera's handbook to find out how it works with various setups.

The Leica Q3 43's included ND filter is a very practical feature that gives you complete creative control over exposure in bright settings. The ND filter allows you more versatility without requiring extra filters or gear, whether you're using it to balance exposure in high contrast settings, photograph wide apertures in sunlight, or create smooth long exposures. Knowing when and how to use it will help you advance your photography by improving your ability to control exposure and light, particularly when the ambient light is too bright for the settings you want.

CHAPTER EIGHT

CREATIVITY AND COMPOSITION IN PHOTOGRAPHY

Utilizing the 35mm, 50mm, and 75mm Digital Crop Modes

Digital Crop Modes (35mm, 50mm, and 75mm) are a useful and effective feature of the Leica Q3 43. With the help of these settings, you can alter your lens's effective focal length without actually altering the lens. You can simulate utilizing multiple focal lengths by cropping the image from the camera's sensor, which will give you more framing options. In many different types of shooting situations, this ability can be immensely helpful.

Digital Crop Modes: What Are They?

The Leica Q3 43's full-frame sensor is used in digital crop modes, which crop the image to replicate the field of view of various focal lengths (35, 50, and 75 mm). In essence, the camera simulates the effect of utilizing many lenses by digitally zooming into the picture to give you a crop. This keeps the image crisp and high-quality while enabling you to construct your shots as though you were using a longer or shorter lens.

The Digital Crop Modes: How Do They Operate?

- **35mm Crop:** To create a 35mm equivalent focal length, the camera crops the middle section of the full-frame image when the 35mm crop mode is selected. In essence, it provides a "zoomed-in" perspective in contrast to the standard 28mm lens.
- **50mm Crop:** By further cropping the sensor, the 50mm crop mode replicates the perspective of a 50mm lens. By doing this, you can shoot at a greater focal length without having to swap out the actual lens.
- **75mm Crop:** By further cropping the image, the 75mm crop mode replicates a telephoto lens. When you need to get closer to a topic without physically moving or switching lenses, this is really helpful.

Digital Crop Modes' Advantages

- **Flexibility without Shifting Perspectives:** The primary benefit of digital crop settings is that they allow you to experiment with different focal lengths without switching lenses. The ability to quickly convert between 35mm, 50mm, and 75mm focal lengths makes it simpler to adjust to different shooting scenarios.

- **Convenience and Simplicity:** Changing lenses can be a pain if you're filming on the go or in a hectic setting. Without physically switching lenses, you may quickly alter your framing to mimic the effect of a different lens with the Leica Q3 43's crop settings.
- **Effectiveness of Shooting:** Occasionally, you might wish to photograph a subject at a longer focal length but lack the time or room to get farther away. You may "zoom in" digitally with the crop modes, giving you greater flexibility in confined situations or when you need to get a close-up of a particular detail.
- **Compact Configuration:** It is also no longer necessary to carry several lenses thanks to the crop modes. You don't need to bring bulky telephoto or zoom lenses because you can mimic various focus lengths. The integrated digital crop modes of the Leica Q3 43 provide you with more reach in a small and lightweight package.

Time to Utilize the Digital Crop Modes

- **Photography on the Street:** In street photography, you frequently have to respond fast to get the scene as it happens. You don't need to physically move or alter your lens to modify the field of view to fit the situation thanks to the 35mm, 50mm, and 75mm crop modes. The 75mm crop mode, for instance, will enable you to digitally zoom in on a person while maintaining the composition if you're strolling through a crowded place and want to take a picture of them from a distance.
- **Photography of Portraits:** Focus length flexibility is useful for portrait photography, particularly for close-up shots. The 50mm crop option is ideal for mimicking the traditional 50mm "look" for a portrait while utilizing the Q3's 28mm lens. Additionally, the 75mm crop mode is a fantastic substitute for conventional portrait lenses if you want a more telephoto feel for closer-up shots.
- **Photography of Landscapes:** Wide vistas or in-depth close-ups are usually what you desire in landscape photography. You may capture a wider perspective while preserving the scene's natural appearance by using the 35mm crop setting. Without physically moving closer or switching lenses, you can use the 50mm or 75mm crop settings to highlight a particular section of your environment.
- **Photographing Wildlife:** It's common for wildlife photographers to have to take long shots without upsetting their subjects. In these cases, the 75mm crop setting is really helpful. It lets you "zoom in" on far-off animals or birds digitally, bringing you closer to your subject without needing to carry or physically approach a long telephoto lens.
- **Photography at Macro Scale:** With a fixed lens, it can occasionally be difficult to get near enough to your subject for macro photography. You may mimic a tighter focal length without physically getting closer by utilizing the digital crop modes. This is particularly useful when you need that extra "zoom" to fill the frame when photographing little subjects, such as flowers or insects.

Digital Crop Modes' Drawbacks

+ **Diminished Resolution:** In essence, you're only using a portion of the full-frame sensor because the digital crop modes crop into the image. Compared to shooting at full sensor size, you may lose some information, but the Leica Q3 43 still produces high-resolution photographs despite the reduced data acquisition.
+ **Diminished Field of View:** Your field of view gets smaller the more you crop. This can be a drawback if you require a wider field of vision for a certain photo because it means that you won't have the same wide perspective as with the native 28mm lens while utilizing the 75mm crop mode.
+ **Considerations after Processing:** You won't be able to crop the image more in post-production without compromising image quality because you're essentially cropping it in the camera. Therefore, it's critical to achieve the best possible composition in the camera.

Taking Pictures at Night and in Low Light

There are special difficulties when shooting at night or in low light, but with the correct methods and conditions, you can produce breathtaking pictures that perfectly convey the beauty of the shadowed world. The Leica Q3 43 has great low-light and night photography skills, whether you're shooting cityscapes, starry skies, or a portrait in a poorly lit space.

Comprehending Photography in Low Light

Any shooting scenario when there is not enough light available for a well-exposed picture under normal conditions is referred to as low light photography. This can include dimly lit interior spaces, sunsets, and nighttime or dusk cityscapes. You will need to modify your camera settings to account for the decreased light levels when shooting in these conditions. **Here's how to accomplish that successfully:**

Enhance ISO Sensitivity

Your camera's sensitivity to light is determined by its ISO. To make the image brighter in low light, you can raise the ISO to let more light reach the sensor. **There is a trade-off with raising the ISO, though, since it may cause noise or grain in the picture.**

+ Use a low ISO (such as 100–400) when the light is brighter or you have more time to expose the picture. An image with less noise and grain is sharper and cleaner when the ISO is lowered.
+ **Higher ISO (e.g., 800-3200):** To obtain a brighter image, you will need to raise the ISO when the light level drops. Higher ISOs are manageable for the Leica Q3 43, particularly when shooting in low light conditions. Start with ISO 800 or 1600, but be aware that very high settings can produce noise.

- **Push ISO to the Limit:** Raise the ISO even farther (3200, 6400, or higher) if you require more light but do not want a slower shutter speed. A brighter image is the result, even though grain may be introduced.

Employ a Wide Aperture

The size of the hole in your lens that lets light reach the sensor is called the aperture. A wider aperture (a lower f-number) will let more light into the camera in low light conditions, making the picture brighter.

- **Wide Aperture (e.g., f/1.4, f/1.8):** When photographing in low light, a wide aperture is crucial because it lets you capture as much light as possible. The fast f/1.7 lens of the Leica Q3 43 is perfect for catching more light and producing bokeh, or lovely, soft backgrounds, in your pictures.
- **Narrow Aperture (f/8, for example):** Unless you have a tripod or are utilizing a very slow shutter speed, stay away from using a narrow aperture in low light. An underexposed photograph could result from a narrow aperture, which will reduce the quantity of light that reaches the sensor.

Slow Shutter Speed

The camera's sensor can record light for a longer amount of time when the shutter speed is lowered. This is crucial for enhancing the picture in low light without raising the ISO too much. Longer shutter speeds, however, also result in motion blur, so keep an eye out for subject movement or camera shake.

- **Extended Exposure (such as 1/30, 1/15, or less):** Your photograph will be brighter and capture more light if you use a slower shutter speed. For nighttime images or to capture fluid motion, such as water or traffic, use long exposures. The Leica Q3 43's integrated image stabilization allows it to withstand extended exposures.
- **Handheld Limitations:** To avoid camera wobble when shooting handheld, choose a shutter speed of at least 1/60 second or faster. A tripod is required for shutter speeds that are slower.

Make use of a tripod

A tripod is necessary for taking pictures at night or with extended exposures. Motion blur may result from even minor movement of the camera because to the increased exposure duration. By keeping the camera stable, a tripod enables you to take crisp, well-exposed pictures free from unwelcome wobble.

Take a RAW picture

RAW format is essential for night and low-light photography. Because RAW files record more information from the sensor, you can make post-processing adjustments to the exposure, white balance, and noise reduction without sacrificing quality. It greatly increases your editing options, particularly in low light situations where you may need to extract features from highlights or shadows.

Leica Q3 43 Night Photography Configurations

You will typically use a mix of slower shutter speeds, a wide aperture, and a higher ISO when shooting at night.

Some recommended settings for several forms of night photography are listed below:

- **For Night Skylines or Cityscapes:**
  - **ISO:** Begin with ISO 1600 or 800.
  - **Aperture:** For a crisp image with a greater depth of field, use f/2.8 or f/4.
  - **Shutter Speed:** To catch city lights and light trails, set a longer exposure (for example, 5–10 seconds).
- **Regarding Astrophotography or Star Photography:**
  - **ISO:** Depending on the amount of light pollution and the noise performance of your camera, choose a higher ISO, such as 3200 or 6400.
  - **Aperture:** Adjust to the widest setting (f/1.7, for example).
  - **Shutter Speed:** To avoid star trails, keep the exposure time between 15 and 30 seconds. You can determine the ideal shutter speed for your focal length by using the 500 rule.
- **For Low-Light Portraits:**
  - **ISO:** To reduce noise, start at ISO 800 or higher if necessary, but don't go overboard.
  - **Aperture:** For soft backgrounds and a shallow depth of field, choose a wide aperture (such as f/1.7).
  - **Shutter Speed:** Unless you're using a tripod, keep it above 1/60 to prevent motion blur.

Employ Focus Peaking or Manual Focus

Autofocus might have trouble in low light, particularly if the scene has little contrast. When shooting in low light, manual focus can be more accurate, and the Leica Q3 43's focus peaking feature makes this possible. You can see precisely where the sharpest portions of your image are by using focus peaking, which highlights the areas that are in focus.

Don't Overexpose Highlights

Certain locations, such as streetlights or bright signs, can quickly become overexposed in nighttime photography. You can prevent overexposing these regions by using the histogram or by looking at the image highlights. To make sure that the bright areas of the picture are evenly distributed, you can use exposure compensation or change the aperture and shutter speed.

Try Out Long Exposure Effects and Light Trails

Experimenting with light trails and long exposure effects is best done at night. Slowing down the shutter speed allows for a lovely capture of motion, whether it's the movement of water, stars in the sky, or automobile lights. Light trails from passing cars or city lights can provide captivating and dramatic compositions that add a creative element to your images.

CHAPTER NINE

CUSTOMIZATION AND ACCESSORIES

SD cards that are suggested for the Q3

To make sure your SD card can handle high-resolution photos, continuous shooting, and video recording, it's crucial to take into account aspects like speed, storage capacity, and dependability when selecting one for your Leica Q3 43. A fast, high-capacity SD card is necessary for the Leica Q3 43's RAW image capture and 4K video recording capabilities.

Important Things to Think About with SD Cards

- Class of Speed:
  - **UHS-I vs. UHS-II:** The Leica Q3 43 is compatible with UHS-I SD cards, but there is also backward compatibility with UHS-II cards. Although UHS-II cards are quicker, the Q3 is unable to take full use of this advantage. Although UHS-I cards are usually more than enough, UHS-II cards may provide extra security if you intend to record in 4K or utilize burst modes frequently.
  - **Speed Rating:** Seek out cards rated Class 10, V30, or U3. These guarantee that video recording and burst photo shooting won't cause delays or frame drops on the card.
- Ability:
  - **Storage:** Since the Leica Q3 43 supports cards up to 512GB, it's wise to pick a card with enough room so you can record 4K video and shoot in RAW without having to swap cards all the time.
  - For daily use, a 64GB or 128GB card should be more than sufficient; however, a 256GB or 512GB card would be better if you intend to take high-resolution photos and videos or conduct extended sessions without changing cards frequently.
- Dependability:
  - Select cards from reputable and well-known brands to guarantee dependability and longevity. Over time, SD cards may degrade, so you want a card that can withstand harsh use (such as prolonged recording sessions or high-speed burst shooting).
  - Seek out cards with a reliability guarantee or a lifetime warranty.

SD cards that are suggested for the Leica Q3 43

- Extreme PRO UHS-I SDXC SanDisk (64GB, 128GB, 256GB, 512GB)
  - **Speed:** Class 10, V30, U3, UHS-I
  - **Read Speed:** 170 MB/s
  - **Write Speed:** 90 MB/s
  - **Capacity:** 64GB, 128GB, 256GB, and 512GB are available.

- ➢ **Why it's great:** SanDisk's Extreme PRO range is renowned for its dependability and quick writing rates. It's a great option for 4K video recording and burst shooting because it strikes a good mix between price and speed.
- ↓ **64GB, 128GB, and 256GB Lexar Professional 1000x UHS-II SDXC**
  - ➢ **Speed:** Class 10, V30, U3, UHS-II
  - ➢ **Reading Speed:** 150 MB/s
  - ➢ **Write Speed:** 90 MB/s
  - ➢ **Capacity:** 64GB, 128GB, and 256GB are available.
  - ➢ **Why it's great:** The Lexar Professional 1000x UHS-II card provides additional headroom for demanding operations, even if the Leica Q3 43 supports UHS-I rates. For those who want to utilize it with UHS-II compliant cameras in the future or who wish to future-proof their setup, it's perfect.
- ↓ **(64GB, 128GB, 256GB) Samsung PRO Endurance UHS-I SDXC**
  - ➢ **Speed:** Class 10, V30, U3, UHS-I
  - ➢ **Reading Speed:** 100 MB/s
  - ➢ **Write Speed:** 30 MB/s
  - ➢ **Capacity:** 64GB, 128GB, and 256GB are available.
  - ➢ **Why it's amazing:** If you intend to record lengthy 4K films or use your Q3 43 for video work, the Samsung PRO Endurance is a perfect choice because it is specifically made for continuous video recording. It has improved wear resistance for long-term dependability and is designed to last.
- ↓ **SDXC UHS-II U3 Transcend (64GB, 128GB, and 256GB)**
  - ➢ **Speed:** Class 10, V90, UHS-II, U3
  - ➢ **Reading Speed:** 285 MB/s
  - ➢ **Write Speed:** 180 MB/s
  - ➢ **Capacity:** 64GB, 128GB, and 256GB are available.
  - ➢ **Why it's amazing:** For people who require speed, particularly for continuous shooting and video recording, the Transcend UHS-II card is a great option. It excels in handling burst photos and high-resolution video, including 4K, without losing frames.
- ↓ **64GB, 128GB, and 256GB Kingston Canvas React plus UHS-II SDXC**
  - ➢ **Speed:** Class 10, V90, UHS-II, U3
  - ➢ **Reading Speed:** 300 MB/s
  - ➢ **Write Speed:** 260 MB/s
  - ➢ **Capacity:** 64GB, 128GB, and 256GB are available.
  - ➢ Why it's great: The Kingston Canvas React Plus is a good choice for high-end video recording, particularly 4K and high-bitrate formats, because it has incredibly fast write speeds. The Q3 43 offers speed and dependability for both video and photo operations, although not fully utilizing UHS-II speeds.
- ↓ **UHS-II SDXC Sony SF-G Tough (64GB, 128GB, 256GB)**
  - ➢ **Speed:** Class 10, V90, UHS-II, U3
  - ➢ **Reading Speed:** 300 MB/s

- ➢ **Write Speed:** 299 MB/s
- ➢ **Capacity:** 64GB, 128GB, and 256GB are available.
- ➢ **Why it's great:** The Sony SF-G Tough is a fantastic option for photographers who prefer to shoot in harsh locations or outdoors because it is designed to endure tough circumstances. One of the quickest SD cards available, it easily manages 4K video and continuous recording.

For the majority of Leica Q3 43 users, a UHS-I card with a V30 or U3 speed rating will be adequate for 4K video recording and high-quality photos. With their speed, capacity, and dependability, cards like the SanDisk Extreme PRO or Lexar Professional 1000x are excellent all-around choices. A UHS-II card, such as the Sony SF-G Tough or Transcend UHS-II U3, can be useful if you need faster read/write speeds or intend to shoot a lot of 4K video, but keep in mind that the Q3 won't be able to fully utilize the UHS-II speeds. Depending on how much you shoot and if you're utilizing RAW image formats or long-form video, a 64GB to 256GB card should be more than enough storage for everyday use. Ultimately, you will be ready to take amazing pictures and videos with your Leica Q3 43 if you select a card from a reliable brand that meets your unique storage, speed, and dependability requirements.

The Greatest Grips, Cases, and Straps

Selecting the appropriate grip, case, and strap for your Leica Q3 43 can greatly enhance your shooting experience. There are many alternatives available that are made to match the streamlined and fashionable appearance of your camera, whether you require extra comfort, protection, or a more secure hold. **Some of the top choices for each of these categories are listed below.**

- ↓ **Leica Q3 43 Straps that Work Best:** When it comes to carrying your Leica Q3 43 in comfort, style, and convenience, a quality strap can make all the difference. **Here are some excellent choices to think about:**
  - ➢ **High-end Leather Shoulder Strap for Leica Camera**

- o **Composition:** Leather
- o **Why it's great:** This high-end leather shoulder strap, made especially for Leica cameras, delivers a stylish and timeless appearance while being comfortable for extended usage. The strap length may be adjusted for the ideal fit, and the supple leather is kind to the skin.

- **Advantages:** comfy, fashionable, and long-lasting. Complements the Leica Q3 43's opulent appearance.
- **Cons:** In order to preserve its appearance over time, leather may require considerable maintenance.

➢ **Strap of Leather with Tap and Dye**

- Full-grain leather is the material.
- **Why it's fantastic:** Tap & Dye is renowned for producing fine, handcrafted leather straps, and their goods are no different. This strap is ideal for people who value style and longevity because it has a high-end feel and superb craftsmanship.
- **Advantages:** incredibly comfy, handcrafted, and adaptable. Additionally, it matures gracefully, acquiring a distinctive patina with time.
- **Cons:** Because it is handcrafted, it is more costly.

➢ **Slide Lite Camera Strap by Peak Design**

- **Composition:** leather and nylon

- o **Why it's great:** The Peak Design Slide Lite is an excellent choice if you'd rather have something more contemporary and adaptable. It has leather accents, soft, long-lasting nylon webbing, and a sliding mechanism that allows you to swiftly change the length of the strap. To equally distribute the weight, the strap also features a fantastic shoulder pad.
- o **Advantages:** incredibly comfy, adjustable, and long-lasting. For easy access to the camera, the sliding method is great.
- o **Drawbacks:** Not as fashionable as leather choices, and less conventional.
- ➢ **The Hard Graft Camera Strap**

- o **Composition:** Wool felt and leather
- o **Reasons for its excellence:** Hard Graft is renowned for creating high-end camera accessories, and their camera straps are no different. This strap is both stylish and useful, combining velvety leather with wool felt for added comfort.
- o **Advantages:** Superior materials, fashionable style, cozy, and distinctive.
- o **Cons:** Expensive pricing.
- ✦ **Optimal Situations for the Leica Q3 43:** A case helps shield your Leica Q3 43 from small bumps, dust, and scratches. Here are some excellent choices for protecting your camera when you're out and about:
  - ➢ **The Leica Always-Ready Case**
    - o **Composition:** Leather
    - o The Leica Ever-Ready Case is excellent since it fits the Leica Q3 43 perfectly and offers stylish protection. It has a cutout for the lens and provides a snug fit around the camera's body.
    - o **Advantages:** Constructed from real leather, it protects the camera and adds a luxurious appearance. Gives you access to every button and dial on the camera.

- o **Drawbacks:** As is common with any fully protected cases, the case's minor bulk can make it a little challenging to use fast.
  - ➢ **Hard Graft Camera Case**
    - o **Composition:** Wool felt and leather
    - o **Why it's fantastic:** A fashionable, premium camera case that will keep your Leica Q3 43 safe. It blends leather and wool felt to provide your camera a smooth, scratch-free surface and a tough, upscale appearance.
    - o **Advantages:** Excellent protection, plush interior and elegant design.
    - o **Drawbacks:** Pricey and designed more as a small carrying case than one for storing extra accessories.
  - ➢ **The Bowery Camera Bag by Ona**
    - o **Composition:** Leather and waxed canvas
    - o **Why it's wonderful:** The Ona the Bowery is a great choice if you're searching for a bag to hold your Leica Q3 43 and a few accessories. You can fit your camera, a few lenses, and tiny accessories in this sleek and small camera bag.
    - o **Advantages:** Elegant, premium materials, neat interior design.
    - o **Cons:** Better suited for light carry, not as protective as hard cases.
  - ➢ **Peak Design 6-Light Daily Sling**
    - o **Composition:** Nylon
    - o **Why it's great:** Your Leica Q3 43 and a few other necessities fit perfectly in this small, cozy sling bag. It's made to give you easy access while protecting your equipment well.
    - o **Benefits:** Excellent organization, fast access, and roomy enough for a small camera bag.
    - o **Drawbacks:** It's better to carry your camera and a few accessories rather than a hard case.
- ✦ **Top Handle Options for the Leica Q3 43:** Enhancing your grip on the Leica Q3 43 with a camera grip can improve comfort, especially when shooting for extended lengths of time, and increase stability for handheld photos.
  - ➢ **Leica Official Q3 Grip**
    - o **Composition:** Aluminum and rubber
    - o **Why it works so well:** This authentic Leica grip is made especially for the Q3, and it fits the camera perfectly. During handheld shooting, it aids with stability and provides a more stable grip, especially in high-action or low-light conditions.
    - o **Advantages:** Personalized, provides a comfortable grip, and preserves the camera's aesthetics.
    - o **Drawbacks:** Pricey for a grip, but long-lasting and aesthetically pleasing to the Q3.
  - ➢ **Thumbs up for grip.**
    - o **Composition:** rubber and aluminum

- o **Why it's great:** The Thumbs Up grip gives your thumb a firm grip by attaching to the camera's hot shoe. For photographers who desire a more ergonomic and comfortable grip without adding bulk, it's a terrific addition.
- o **Benefits:** Excellent for increasing comfort and grip. Lightweight and unaffected by the size of the camera.
- o **Drawbacks:** Provides less grasp than a full grip, particularly for larger-handed individuals.
- ➢ **Grip and Soft Release Button**
  - o **Composition:** Soft rubber
  - o **Why it's great:** Including a little rubber grip around the shutter button and a soft release button improves tactile feedback and facilitates taking accurate pictures. This is a fantastic method to enhance your shooting experience without significantly increasing the camera's bulk.
  - o **Benefits:** Affordable, enhances the feel of the shutter release, and is comfortable.
  - o **Drawbacks:** Not as physically gripping as comparable full-size grips.
- ➢ **Gariz Grip-equipped Half Leather Case**
  - o **Composition:** Plastic and leather
  - o **Why it's great:** The Gariz Half Leather Case offers a built-in grip that makes it easier to hold the Leica Q3 43, especially when shooting for extended periods of time, in addition to offering superb protection for the camera. The camera's appearance is further improved by the leather.
  - o **Advantages:** Lightweight, integrated grip, premium leather.
  - o **Drawbacks:** Not as sturdy as a complete grip, and because of the leather, it may cost a little more.

Your experience with the Leica Q3 43 can be substantially improved by selecting the appropriate grip, case, and strap. There are many of excellent solutions available, whether you're searching for a protective case, a fashionable leather strap, or a comfortable grip. Think about your shooting patterns, personal preferences, and camera carrying style. There is the ideal accessory to go with your Leica Q3 43 and improve your shooting setup, whatever of your priorities for comfort, security, or style.

External Lighting and Flash Devices

Whether you're shooting indoors, in low light, or simply want to have greater control over how light strikes your subject, the purpose of using external flash and lighting accessories with the Leica Q3 43 is to improve your lighting setup. Like many other cameras, the Q3 includes built-in features that may be enhanced by external flashes and light modifiers. If you know how to utilize these tools well, you can dramatically improve your photography.

External Flash

It's crucial to comprehend the range of possibilities on the market when thinking about external flashes for your Leica Q3 43. Every flash has different characteristics, and the type of setting you shoot in, your preferred amount of lighting control, and your photographic style will all influence your choice. **Popular external flashes are listed and explained in depth below, along with information on their advantages and particular applications.**

The Godox V1

Unlike square-headed flashes, which have a crisp, direct flash, the Godox V1 is a well-liked external flash with a circular head that simulates the light quality of a continuous light source. The Godox V1's spherical head allows for a more natural light fall-off, which is perfect for portraiture, where softer light is frequently preferred.

Important Features

+ **Round Head:** For portraiture, the round head produces a softer, more pleasant light by distributing light more evenly and minimizing harsh shadows.
+ **High Power (GN 92):** With a strong guide number of 92, this flash has more than enough power to illuminate huge objects or operate in larger areas.
+ It is excellent for rapid shooting and synchronization with fast shutter rates because to its TTL (Through the Lens) and HSS (High-Speed Sync) functions.
+ **Rechargeable Battery:** The Godox V1 has a lithium-ion battery, which offers quicker recycling times, a longer battery life, and more reliable performance during a shot than many other flashes that use AA batteries.
+ **Wireless Capability:** You may position your light source more creatively with wireless triggers, allowing you to use it off-camera.

Why the Leica Q3 benefits greatly from it

The Godox V1's adaptability and user-friendliness make it a great option for the Leica Q3. It is a good choice for both novice and experienced photographers due to its high power, quick recycle time, and simple controls. You can also use it remotely thanks to its wireless feature, which eliminates the need to position the flash directly on the camera.

The Profoto B10

High-end lighting manufacturer Profoto is renowned for creating flashes with performance and quality comparable to those of professionals. For portrait and product photographers who require strong lighting without a large setup, the Profoto B10 is the perfect flash because it is small, portable, and produces amazing light output.

Important Features

- **Compact Size:** The Profoto B10 is one of the smallest studio lights on the market, which making it incredibly portable and simple to use on site even with its strong output.
- **Guide Number of 76:** The B10 has a high guide number, meaning it has enough power for practically every circumstance, particularly in portrait and studio photography.
- **TTL, HSS, and Continuous Light:** The B10 has the same TTL and HSS as other flashes, but it's perfect for still and video photography because it can also be used as a continuous light source.
- **Wireless Control:** Even when the flash is off-camera, you can still obtain the illumination you want by using the Profoto Air Remote to remotely control and modify the B10's light output.

Why the Leica Q3 benefits greatly from it

The Profoto B10 is a fantastic addition to your Leica Q3 if you're searching for something sturdy and adaptable. It is easy to use both on location and in the studio because of its amazing light output in a compact, portable form. The B10 provides a dual solution for photographers who require both flash and continuous light options.

The Nikon SB-700

Despite being primarily made for Nikon cameras, the Nikon SB-700 can still be utilized with the Leica Q3 over Bluetooth or compatible wireless triggering systems. Despite being one of Nikon's more reasonably priced flashes, it is nevertheless very powerful, versatile, and user-friendly.

Important Features

The SB-700 has a good level of flash power, making it appropriate for most indoor or small outdoor sessions. Its guide number is 28 (at 35mm). **Although it isn't as strong as some of the other flashes on this list, it works well in the majority of circumstances.**

- **Swivel and tilt:** By rotating and tilting the flash head, you may bounce light off ceilings and walls to create softer, more organic lighting.
- **TTL and HSS:** The SB-700 is a dependable instrument for dynamic situations requiring fast adjustments because it offers TTL metering and high-speed sync.
- **Integrated Bounce Card:** When you wish to further soften the light, the integrated bounce card is a fantastic complement for dispersing the flash.

Why it works well with the Leica Q3

For those seeking a flash that offers the required control without going over budget, the Nikon SB-700 is a dependable and reasonably priced choice. If you're seeking to add exterior lighting on a budget, this multipurpose tool works well with the Q3, even though it's not as strong as other more expensive options.

Speedlite 600EX II-RT from Canon

Although it is made for Canon cameras, the top-tier Canon Speedlite 600EX II-RT flash can be utilized with the Leica Q3 using compatible wireless networks. For serious photographers who want strong exterior lighting, this flash is a good option because it provides professional-grade features and performance.

Important Features

- **Guide Number of 60:** The 600EX II-RT's strong guide number makes it appropriate for larger venues or scenarios requiring a lot of light output, such events or studio shoots.
- **Wireless Slave and Master Modes:** This flash has wireless control, so you can set it away from the camera and manage its output from a distance.
- **HSS and TTL:** Even in hectic shooting situations, high-speed sync and TTL metering offer superb control over flash exposure.
- **Durability:** The 600EX II-RT is made to last because to its water and dust resistance, which makes it perfect for use in outdoor photography or more demanding environments.

Why it works so well with the Leica Q3

The Canon Speedlite 600EX II-RT is a fantastic option if you're searching for something with features of a professional caliber. Its strong light output, dependable wireless operation, and superb control all enhance the Leica Q3's capabilities, particularly for studio or event photography.

Yongnuo YN560 IV

The Yongnuo YN560 IV is a reliable external flash that provides excellent value for people on a smaller budget. Even though it doesn't have the sophisticated capabilities like TTL and HSS that more costly flash have, it still offers a lot of power and versatility, which makes it a popular option for novice off-camera flash users or amateur photographers on a tight budget who require dependable lighting.

Important Features

- **Guide Number of 58:** This flash's guide number of 58 indicates that it has sufficient power for the majority of indoor and portrait photography. Photographers searching for a powerful yet reasonably priced flash alternative will find it especially helpful.
- **Manual Mode:** The YN560 IV functions in manual mode, in contrast to more costly flashes with TTL. This provides you total control over the illumination, but it also means you'll have to manually regulate the flash power.
- **Wireless Control:** With suitable wireless triggers, the flash can be used off-camera thanks to its wireless master and slave modes.
- **Cost-effective:** The YN560 IV is among the least expensive solutions on the market while maintaining a high degree of power and adaptability.

Why it works so well with the Leica Q3

The Yongnuo YN560 IV is an excellent, reasonably priced choice that offers you a great deal of manual control freedom. It's ideal for photographers who are new to using external flashes or who feel comfortable adjusting their own flash output.

Wireless Triggers

A wireless trigger device is required if you wish to use your external flash off-camera for more imaginative lighting. You may place the flash anywhere you want without worrying about cords thanks to these gadgets, which enable communication between your camera and the flash without a physical connection.

- **Radio Frequency Triggers:** These may penetrate furniture and walls and are more dependable over greater distances. Generally speaking, their consistency and range are superior.
- **Infrared Triggers:** If you're working in a well-lit area with unobstructed vision, you can use these. Although they are typically less costly, they may not be as dependable across bigger areas or in the presence of obstacles.

Lighting Add-ons

The quality and ambiance of your lighting can be significantly altered by adding accessories to your flash. If you want to better manage your light and achieve certain styles, these accessories are a must. **Here are a few typical accessories to think about:**

- **Diffusers:** By dispersing the light from the flash, a diffuser—a soft substance that is frequently translucent—softens harsh shadows and produces more uniform lighting. When employing the flash near your topic, they are quite helpful. For more control, you can purchase separate diffusers, but some flashes have them built in.
- **Softboxes:** A light modifier that produces gentle, diffused light is called a softbox. These are especially helpful for portrait photography since they reduce harsh shadows and make the subject's skin appear more attractive. There are many sizes of softboxes; larger ones give off a softer, more organic appearance.
- **Reflectors:** Shadows can be filled in by using reflectors to bounce light back onto your subject. In portrait photography, these are particularly helpful for highlighting the dark parts of the face without the need for an additional light source. Reflectors are available in a variety of colors, including gold, silver, and white, and each one reflects light in a unique way.
- **Gels:** To alter the color temperature of the light, you can attach colored filters called gels to your flash. This is helpful when you want to produce a creative, colorful look or when you want to adjust the flash to ambient illumination (such as tungsten or daylight lighting settings).
- **Barn Doors:** You may adjust the form and direction of the light by using barn doors, a kind of flag that fastens to the front of your flash or light source. They are especially helpful when you want to focus light on a single spot without letting it flow onto the background or other elements of your picture.
- **Grid Locations:** You have more control over where the light falls thanks to an attachment called a grid spot, which narrows the light beam. They produce a spotlight effect, which is excellent for specific product photography or dramatic portraits.

- **Umbrellas:** Another traditional light modulator that may be utilized in a variety of ways to bounce or soften light is an umbrella. For a softer, more diffused light, use a shoot-through umbrella; alternatively, use a reflecting umbrella to bounce the flash light back onto your subject. These may produce quite beautiful and natural lighting and are simple to set up.

Using Lens Hoods and Filters

With your Leica Q3 43, using filters and lens hoods can greatly improve your photos while providing both useful and artistic opportunities. These add-ons lessen undesired reflections, regulate the amount of light that enters the lens, and shield it from harm. Whether you're shooting landscapes, portraits, or something else entirely, knowing how to use these tools well will help you produce photographs that are on par with the best.

About Filters

Accessories called filters fit on the front of your lens and alter light before it enters the sensor. There are several varieties of them, and each has a distinct function. **The most popular filter types and their applications with the Leica Q3 are as follows:**

The UV Filter

The main purpose of UV filters is to prevent ultraviolet radiation from getting to your lens. UV filters are still widely used for their protective properties even though contemporary digital sensors are not as sensitive to UV light as film. They aid with preventing dust, grime, scratches, and unintentional damage to the front of your lens. Additionally, photographers who shoot outside frequently employ UV filters because they assist minimize atmospheric haze in landscape photographs, particularly in coastal or higher elevation settings.

Principal Advantages

- **Lens Protection:** UV filters serve as a barrier to protect your lens's front component from unintentional scratches or bumps.
- **Less Haze:** They are a wonderful option for landscape photography since they can lessen haze in outdoor images, especially in bright, clear circumstances.

Cons

Minimal Impact on Image Quality: Although the UV filter has a negligible effect, some photographers believe it can cause subtle color shifts or reduce image clarity, particularly at high resolutions.

Polarizing filters

When taking pictures outside, a polarizing filter is an excellent tool for reducing glare and reflections. Because it is a rotating circular filter, you may change how strong the polarizing effect is. This is particularly useful when taking pictures of glass, water, or damp surfaces because reflections can be distracting. It also improves the color of skies, giving them a more rich appearance and lessening the washed-out appearance that intense sunlight can cause.

Principal Advantages

- **Reducing Glare and Reflections:** It can reduce glare and reflections from glass, water, and other sparkling surfaces, improving the clarity of your photos.
- **Enhanced Contrast:** By emphasizing clouds and darkening blue skies, a polarizing filter can add depth and contrast to your landscape photographs.
- **Better Color Saturation:** Your landscape and nature photographs look more appealing overall as colors, especially greens and blues, become brighter.

Cons

Needs Rotation: In order to get the desired effect, you must rotate the filter, which can be difficult in some shooting situations. Additionally, when filming at wider angles, the effect might not be as noticeable.

Filters with Neutral Density (ND)

ND filters are crucial instruments for managing exposure, particularly in bright environments or when achieving specific artistic effects. By reducing the quantity of light that enters the lens, an ND filter essentially enables you to use wider apertures or longer shutter speeds even during the day. This can be perfect for getting a shallow depth of focus in direct sunshine or for shooting motion-blurred, smooth water.

Principal Advantages

- **Control Exposure:** ND filters are ideal for increasing aperture or decreasing shutter speed without overexposing your photos. For instance, a longer exposure can be used to capture smooth, flowing waterfalls, or intense lighting can produce a shallow depth of field.
- **Enable Creative Effects:** They're excellent for enabling creative photography in dynamic settings and producing long-exposure effects, even during the day.

Cons

+ **Potential Color Shift:** Some inferior ND filters may cause your photos to have a color cast that needs to be fixed in post-production.

Filters with graduated ND

Similar to a standard ND filter, a graduated ND filter lets you manage exposure in particular areas of the picture by gradually changing from dark to light. This helps equalize the exposure between the two, which is especially helpful when taking pictures of landscapes with brilliant skies and darker ground. A graded ND filter, for instance, helps preserve the foreground well-lit while preventing overexposure of the bright sky when photographing a sunset or sunrise.

Principal Advantages

+ **Exposure Balance:** In landscape photography in particular, graduated ND filters aid in balancing exposure between the darker ground and bright sky.
+ **Preserve Highlights:** They can stop the sky's highlights from blowing out, which is particularly helpful in bright daylight or golden hour.

Cons

+ **Limited Use:** Not all circumstances call for the use of these filters. They function best when the sky and ground have a noticeable variation in brightness or when there is a distinct horizon line.

Color Filters

In black-and-white photography, color filters are commonly employed to modify the tonal contrast between various hues. For instance, in black-and-white landscape photos, a yellow or orange filter can enhance contrast, while a red filter can darken skies and highlight clouds. They are nevertheless useful in some artistic situations or to achieve a retro effect, even if they are not frequently utilized in digital color photography.

Principal Advantages

+ **Produce Dramatic Effects:** By adding warmth or coldness to your photos, color filters can help you convey a particular tone or emotion.
+ **Improve Black-and-White photos:** They are quite useful for changing the contrast between various colors in black-and-white photos.

Cons

+ **Restricted to Black-and-White Photography:** Color filters are rarely applied to digital color photographs and are most helpful in black-and-white photography.

Lens Hoods

Attaching to the front of your lens, a lens hood is a necessary device that reduces lens flare and protects it from stray light. In addition, it is a cheap method of protecting your lens from scratches and other physical disturbances. Lens hoods are essential for enhancing the quality and durability of your images, even though many photographers concentrate on filters to improve image quality.

Principal Advantages

+ **Reducing Lens Flare:** One of a lens hood's most crucial roles is to stop lens flare, which is brought on by light striking your lens's front element at an oblique angle. Flare can cause your photos to have unwelcome bright patches, haze, and less contrast.
+ **Better Contrast and Color:** Lens hoods enhance contrast and color saturation by obstructing stray light, guaranteeing that your photos are vibrant and clear without the washed-out appearance brought on by light leaking into the lens.
+ **Physical Protection:** Lens hoods shield the front of your lens from unintentional harm by adding an additional layer of defense against bumps, dust, and rain.

Lens hood types include:

+ **Petal (Flower) Shaped:** Wide-angle lenses frequently employ these hoods. Wide views are ideal since the petals provide optimum protection without disturbing the image frame.
+ **Round Shaped:** These hoods offer consistent protection around the lens and are more frequently found for telephoto lenses. They are perfect for keeping a small form factor while lowering flare.

Why Should the Leica Q3 Be Used with a Lens Hood?

Stray light and flare can more obviously affect the quality of your images because the Leica Q3 features a high-resolution sensor that can capture a lot of detail. When photographing outside in bright light or when facing direct light sources, such as the sun, using a lens hood helps preserve the sharpness and clarity of your images.

CHAPTER TEN
ABOUT MAINTENANCE AND DEBUGGING
How to Maintain and Clean Your Leica Q3 43

Maintaining your Leica Q3 43's functionality and making sure it lasts for many years requires regular cleaning and protection. In addition to keeping the camera body and lens appearing brand new, proper maintenance also helps maintain the quality of your photos. Even though the Leica Q3 is a sturdy and well-made camera, maintaining its longevity and obtaining the greatest performance may be achieved with routine cleaning and care.

Cleaning the Body of the Camera

The Leica Q3's camera body is constructed from premium materials, such as magnesium alloy, and is intended to endure regular use. Dust, grime, and moisture can still build up, though, and over time, these could harm internal parts. To start cleaning the camera's exterior, turn it off and take out the battery to prevent inadvertent button pushes or power drains. Wipe the camera body's surface lightly using a microfiber cloth. Because microfiber is soft and won't scratch the surface, it's perfect. If the dirt is difficult to remove, you can dab the cloth with water or a gentle lens cleaning solution, but stay away from harsh chemicals or abrasives as these might harm the finish. Particular attention should be paid to places like buttons, dials, and ports where dust can readily gather. To remove debris around these locations without running the risk of scratching or breaking the camera, a soft brush or blower can be helpful. Use a blower to get rid of any dust when cleaning the lens mount. Avoid putting your hands directly on the lens mount because this might leave smudges that are hard to get rid of.

Lens Cleaning

Since the lens is undoubtedly the most crucial component of your camera, maintaining its cleanliness is essential to producing crisp, high-quality photos. Unwanted blur or soft patches may appear in your images due to dust, fingerprints, or smudges on the lens. You should first use a blower to get rid of any loose particles before cleaning the lens. To prevent scratching the lens surface, do this lightly. Then, if required, wipe the lens using a lens tissue or microfiber cloth. To prevent streaks or uneven cleaning, always wipe the lens in a circular motion, working your way outward from the center. You can use a tiny bit of lens cleaning solution made especially for camera lenses to softly moisten the cloth in the event of oil smudges or obstinate fingerprints. Applying too much liquid could cause too much moisture to infiltrate into the lens housing. After cleaning, make sure there is no moisture left on the lens by wiping it again with a dry portion of the towel.

Keeping the Lens Safe

When not in use, always keep the lens covered to avoid dust, fingerprints, and scratches building up on it. To cover the lens's front element, a lens cap is necessary. Additionally, think about adding a UV or transparent filter on the lens when shooting in areas with dampness or dust. This serves as an additional line of defense against moisture, dust, and scratches that could damage the lens itself. It's crucial to remember that these filters, like the lens, can get dirty and should be maintained clean. Using a lens hood is an additional method of lens protection. A lens hood provides a certain amount of physical protection against bumps, drops, and unintentional scratches when you're handling or storing the camera, even if its main purpose is to stop lens flare from direct sunlight. To guarantee a secure fit and efficient protection, use the lens hood that is compatible with your Leica Q3 lens.

Keeping the Camera Body Safe

Although the Leica Q3 is built to last, it's wise to take some extra safety measures to safeguard your investment. When not in use, keep your camera safe from moisture, dust, and impacts by keeping it in a well-padded camera case. Additionally, you want to think about spending money on a protective case or skin, which can provide an extra degree of defense without detracting from the camera's elegant appearance. Photographers who take their cameras outside or on trips where the camera may be subjected to more adverse conditions may find these cases extremely helpful. It's important to keep the camera as dry as possible when shooting in humid or rainy situations. Despite being weather-sealed, the Leica Q3 should still be protected from direct water exposure. When caught in rainy weather, make sure the camera is protected by using a rain cover or a camera bag with water-resistant materials.

Memory cards and batteries

Maintaining the battery and memory cards is just as crucial as cleaning the camera's body and optics. To prevent any possible drain, always take the camera's battery out while not in use for a long time. Use a dry microfiber cloth to carefully wipe the battery contacts to keep them clean. Memory cards need to be handled with care and stored dust-free. Use a gentle blower to carefully remove any debris from the card slots if necessary. Cards that look unclean should not be inserted because this can harm the card and the camera slot.

Typical Problems and Solutions

Like any sophisticated piece of gear, the Leica Q3 43 may periodically have problems that could impair its functionality. Don't worry; most of these issues can be resolved with a little tinkering. **They can range from small annoyances to more complicated difficulties.**
   - **The Camera Is Not Turning On:** One of the most frequent problems you may encounter is this one. Here are some things to look for, since it might be a straightforward solution or a sign of a more serious issue.

- > **Possible Reasons and Solutions:**
  - ▪ **Battery Problems:** The battery is the most evident source. Verify that the battery is inserted correctly. The camera could not turn on if the battery is not placed properly. To make sure the battery is in position, try taking it out and putting it back in.
    - o **Fix:** Take out and fully charge the battery if it is correctly inserted but still does not turn on. It could be necessary to replace the battery if it isn't retaining a charge.
    - o **Advice:** For optimal performance, always use the original Leica battery. Batteries from third parties might not perform as well.
  - ▪ **Battery Corrosion or Dirt:** The camera may not switch on if the battery contacts are corroded or dusty.
    - o **Repair:** To make sure there is no dust or corrosion, gently wipe the battery contacts with a cotton swab or a dry microfiber cloth.
  - ▪ Power Button Not Responding: Dust or dirt may be causing the power button to become stuck or not register. Although uncommon, this can occur.
    - o **Solution:** Try gently pressing the power Button a few times to see if it unsticks, or clean the area around it with a soft brush.
- ✦ **The camera becomes unresponsive or freezes:** A software error, a stalled operation, or an overloaded memory card could be the cause of your Leica Q3 freezing or becoming unresponsive while in use.
  - > **Possible Reasons and Solutions:**
    - ▪ **Frozen Software:** The firmware of the camera may occasionally freeze, making it incapable of reacting to inputs.
      - o **Solution:** Try turning the camera on and off once more. If it doesn't work, take out the battery, wait a short while, then put it back in and switch the camera back on.
    - ▪ **Memory Card Problems:** The camera may freeze if the memory card is full or corrupted. The camera may hang or stop responding if it is having trouble writing to the card.
      - o **Solution:** Take out the memory card, make sure it's inserted correctly, and make sure it's not full. Try formatting the camera's memory card (be sure to back-up your images first if needed) or getting a new one.
    - ▪ **Firmware Issues:** Outdated firmware might occasionally result in poor performance. Make sure the firmware on your camera is always up to date.
      - o **Fix:** To see if your model has a firmware update available, go to Leica's website. If so, install the update by following the given steps.
- ✦ **Images that are blurry or out of focus:** Focus problems, camera motion, or improper settings are frequently the causes of blurry photos. Determining if the issue is with the camera, lens, or settings is crucial.

> **Possible Reasons and Solutions:**
>   - **Auto-Focus Issues:** Low contrast, bad lighting, or a problem with the autofocus technology could be the cause of the camera's difficulty focusing on your subject.
>   - **Fix:** Make sure you're looking at a bright, contrasted location. Sharpen the image by adjusting the focus ring and switching to manual focus if needed.
>   - **Camera Shake:** If you're not using a tripod, camera shake can easily result in blurry photos when shooting at reduced shutter speeds.
>   - **Fix:** Use a tripod for greater stability or increase the shutter speed to reduce the likelihood of the camera shaking. If in-camera stabilization is available, you can also activate it.
>   - **Incorrect Settings:** Occasionally, merely having the camera settings off will result in fuzzy photographs. This can entail setting the ISO too high, the shutter speed too low, or the aperture too wide.
>   - To fix this, make sure your shutter speed, aperture, and ISO settings are suitable for your subject and lighting. Aim for a shutter speed of at least 1/60th of a second when shooting handheld, depending on the lens's focal length.
- **Not Firing Flash:** There are a number of reasons why your Leica Q3's flash could not be activating when you hit the shutter. Particularly when using external flash units or certain settings, the built-in flash might be problematic.
    > **Possible Reasons and Solutions:**
    >   - **Flash Disabled:** Verify in the camera's settings that the flash is off. It's simple to inadvertently turn off the flash in the control settings or disable it in the menu.
    >   - **Solution:** Verify that the flash is turned on in the menu of your camera. Make sure the external flash is turned on and connected correctly if you're using one.
    >   - **Battery Power:** The camera might not have enough power to activate the flash if its battery is low.
    >   - **Solution:** Verify that your battery is fully charged. Verify the battery life of the external flash if you're using one.
    >   - **Flash Sync Speed:** Due to sync speed constraints, the flash could not fire if you are utilizing high-speed shutter settings.
    >   - **Fix:** Set your shutter speed so that it matches the pace at which your flash syncs. Most cameras have a maximum sync speed of 1/200 or 1/250 seconds, though this might change depending on the settings.
- **Low Image Quality (Artifacts, Color Cast, or Noise):** Your settings, ISO levels, or post-processing may be the source of noise, color shifts, or visual artifacts in your photos.
    > **Possible Reasons and Solutions:**
    >   - **High ISO Settings:** Using high ISO settings, particularly those above 1600 or 3200, might cause noise to be introduced into your photos, lowering their quality.

- o **Fix:** To improve image quality, reduce the ISO settings. Try using a tripod if you must take pictures in low light to prevent needlessly raising the ISO.
- **White Balance Problems:** Your photos may appear too warm or too cold due to color casts caused by improper white balance settings.
  - o **Fix:** Manually adjust the white balance according to the conditions in which you are shooting (e.g., Daylight, Cloudy, Tungsten). Shooting in RAW allows you to modify the white balance in post-processing.
- **Lens Aberrations or Artifacts:** Image quality can occasionally be impacted by lens problems such as chromatic aberration (color fringing) or other artifacts, particularly around the frame's edges.
  - o **Fix:** Post-processing software frequently fixes these problems. If you observe recurring problems with a certain lens, look for physical deterioration or cleaning concerns; the lens may require maintenance or repair.

- **Error Notifications or Camera Issues:** A broken internal system or incompatible settings may be the cause of the Leica Q3's malfunction if it shows an error message or starts acting strangely in other ways.
  - ➤ **Possible Reasons and Solutions:**
    - **System Error:** A reset or firmware upgrade may be necessary if you observe a system error or if the camera does not function as intended.
      - o **Solution:** Switch off the camera, take out the battery, give it a minute, and then put it back in. Check for firmware updates or use the menu to return the camera to its original settings if the problem continues.
    - **Memory Card Error:** Error messages may also be caused by a memory card problem.
      - o **Repair:** Take out the memory card, check it for damage, and put it back in. Try formatting the memory card or using a different card if the issue persists.

Tips and Management for Battery Life

When using your Leica Q3 43, battery life is a crucial consideration, particularly for lengthy shoots or when you're on location and don't have easy access to recharge stations. Although the Leica Q3's battery performs rather well, you can make sure you get the most out of each charge by managing your battery properly and using it efficiently. The finest strategies and advice for efficiently controlling battery life are shown below.

Track How Much Battery You're Using

Knowing how much power you're using and how to extend its lifespan is the first step in managing battery life. The screen of the Leica Q3 has a battery level indicator, which is helpful for monitoring your remaining charge. It's crucial to have a plan in place for either power conservation or battery replacement when your battery is getting low.

Advice: Battery %: Develop the practice of routinely checking the battery %, particularly prior to lengthy shoots. If the percentage is less than 20%, think about bringing an extra battery or, if one is available, going to a charging station.

Disable Power-Hungry Functions

Although helpful, a number of camera capabilities have the potential to rapidly deplete your battery. **You may prolong the life of your battery by shutting them off or minimizing their use. Some of the more power-hungry features are as follows:**

Managing Power-Hungry Features

- **Wi-Fi and Bluetooth:** To conserve battery life, it's preferable to turn off Wi-Fi and Bluetooth when not in use, such as for remote control or picture transfer. These features use power and are always looking for connections.
- **LCD Screen Brightness:** One of the primary sources of battery depletion is the LCD screen. You may save a lot of power by dimming the screen or shutting it off when not in use.
- **Live View:** Compared to using the viewfinder, using the camera's live view or continuous autofocus uses more power. To save battery life, use the viewfinder whenever you can.

Advice: The screen's automatic turn-off time can be changed in the camera settings to have it shut off after a brief period of inactivity. This helps cut down on wasteful electricity use.

Disable Image Stabilization

An image stabilization mechanism on the Leica Q3 aids in taking crisp pictures, particularly in dim lighting. But while this system is operating, it uses more energy. To save battery life, you can disable the image stabilization function if you're using a tripod or are shooting in well-lit areas.

Advice: Only employ image stabilization when required. To preserve battery life, switch off stabilization if you're shooting on a tripod or in an environment where camera wobble isn't a problem.

Employ Power-Saving Settings

Leica frequently adds power-saving features to its camera settings in an effort to prolong battery life. To automatically change specific features to use less power, such lowering the focusing strength or dimming the screen, you can turn on the Q3's "power-saving mode" or a similar setting.

Advice: During your shoot, always check the settings menu for any power-saving options that might be activated.

Instead of using the LCD screen, use the viewfinder

Although it's more handy, utilizing the LCD screen to compose your photographs uses up your battery more quickly than using the viewfinder. In addition to using less power, the viewfinder is a more energy-efficient choice if you're in a bright area where the LCD might be difficult to see anyhow.

Advice: To save battery life, use the electronic viewfinder (if one is provided) when taking pictures, especially in bright light.

Keep extra batteries on hand

Carrying extra batteries is usually a good idea, especially for extended sessions or when you're going to places where charging could be challenging. A few extra batteries in your bag can prevent you from running out of power in the middle of a shot because the Leica Q3 utilizes a particular type of battery.

Advice: Properly Store Spare Batteries: To guard against damage and unintentional draining, keep your spare batteries in a protected case.

On-the-Go Charging

It can be difficult to charge your battery when you're on the go. Nonetheless, there are a number of ways to charge your Leica Q3 in various circumstances:

Transportable Power Bank

- **Portable Power Banks:** Recharging your battery while on the go is made easy with a portable power bank. Numerous power banks are small and capable of charging both cellphones and cameras. Make sure the voltage and output of the power bank you select match those of your camera.

Car Charger

- **Car Charger:** A car charger that matches your camera's charging port is a practical method to keep your batteries charged while you're traveling, especially if you're going on a road trip or shooting in places where you'll be in the car for extended periods of time.

Advice

- **Charge Overnight:** To ensure that your batteries are completely charged for the following day of shooting, charge them overnight while you're at home or in a hotel. To prevent any possible harm to the battery or camera, always use the original Leica charger.

Make use of the camera's auto-off feature

The Leica Q3 is one of many contemporary cameras that have an auto power-off option that will switch the camera off on its own after a certain period of inactivity. By doing this, you can prevent unintentionally leaving your camera on and depleting the battery.

Advice: Choose a brief interval, such as one or two minutes, for the auto power-off time. By doing this, you can save electricity without having to manually switch off the camera each time you finish a shot.

Properly charge batteries

To increase battery life over time, proper maintenance is essential. The Q3's lithium-ion batteries work best when kept between 20% and 80% charged, so try not to let them run entirely flat. Additionally, if you're not using the camera, avoid leaving the battery in it for long periods of time as this may cause needless power consumption.

Advice:

- **Prevent Overcharging:** To prevent overcharging, disconnect the battery from the charger as soon as it is fully charged. Even if the majority of contemporary cameras guard against overcharging, it's still a good idea to unplug the charger as soon as the battery is full.

Disable Superfluous Camera Features

The battery may also be depleted by some camera functions, such GPS tagging or automatic image assessment. Think about shutting them off if you are not using them.

Advice:

- **Image Review:** Either disable or shorten the automated image review time (the screen that displays the photo you just took).
- **GPS:** To save battery life, turn off your camera if it uses GPS tagging or location services, especially if you aren't utilizing it to geotag your images.

Being aware of the settings and routines that consume the most power is the key to managing the battery life of your Leica Q3. You may greatly increase battery life by modifying settings like Wi-Fi, image stabilization, and screen brightness as well as by disabling unused features. You won't ever run out of power during a shoot if you have extra batteries on hand and use charging devices like car chargers or portable power banks. By keeping these pointers in mind, you can make the most of your Leica Q3 and take stunning pictures without worrying about running out of battery.

CHAPTER ELEVEN
THE EXPERT TIPS AND TECHNIQUES
Taking Street Photos with the Q3 43

We street photographers were given a new tool with the release of the Leica Q3 43. It is a refreshing change that the 43mm lens has a smaller field of view than the superb 28mm Q lens. For street photographers like me, it works wonderfully. Leica's Q-series cameras are great, but I would much rather be a little farther away from the subject.

I can now confidently claim that the new 43mm APO-Summicron lens is excellent. It's hard to top because it can automatically target, blur, sharpen, and adjust brightness. My "preferred" method for taking street photography is to attempt to capture the subject in a natural setting. But when the opportunity arises, I will also speak with others. I always warn people not to stare at the camera when I'm taking their picture. I avoid taking pictures of people who I know will be upset.

Street photographer's camera settings

After considerable consideration, I concluded that the following setup is the most effective approach for street photographers to utilize this camera's features and lens for impromptu street photos:

- Auto ISO with a 1/250 s minimum shutter speed
- Multi-field exposure metering
- Exposure compensation is set to -0.7 in order to preserve the highlights.
- Auto exposure with aperture priority, with the lens at f/2 or f/2.8. High shutter speeds are frequently the outcome, which the electronic shutter manages well.
- The lens is set to autofocus.
- The Auto Focus mode Body, Face, and Eye Detection
- Despite popular belief, macro lens mode has its uses. View the example of a copy below.

To ensure that I wouldn't make any mistakes when setting up the camera, I created a user persona named "STREET". You seldom ever need to use manual focus because the camera has autofocus. Even at f/2, I've discovered that the AF typically captures the subject's face in the ideal focus. If I have more than one photograph, I will stop down to f/2.8 or f/4 to acquire the proper depth of field. The subject is distinguished from the backdrop and the bokeh looks fantastic because to the tiny depth of field in these images.

Picture framing

I'm carrying the Q3 43. It normally takes too long to grab the camera when you hang it by your side. The best technique to snap a quick photo is to use the EVF. Like myself, many street shooters wear non-polarized sunglasses to improve their vision of the EVF. **Two additional abilities should be practiced by anyone who wants to become a proficient street shooter:**

- **Taking a hip-shot:** To develop an appropriate aim, this requires practice. It is preferable to be farther away in order to account for the inevitable framing flaws and better capture the subject.
- Using the rear LCD screen rather than the EVF to frame the image. Although it's a little less evident than utilizing the EVF, here is a simple method that might work. It's helpful that the Q3 LCD rear screen may be expanded widely.

About Add-ons

I prefer to have a firm grip when I'm carrying a camera. I hold the Q3 with both hands and my thumb. You need to wear a wrist strap or a neck strap over your wrist to prevent a horrible fall. A bag or an elegant case? Thank you. Lightweight cameras are ideal for street photography. When you're ready to shoot, the camera will be secure in a rubberized pouch. You may then roll it up and store it out of the way in your pocket. My Leica Neoprene Case M is this one. It features a few more SD card slots and fits nicely. The camera's included lens hood is a great little device. However, I discovered that using a filter on the lens does not allow you to pick the macro lens mode. This is because the lens hood is interfering. I am aware that Leica will be releasing a redesigned hood in the future to address this problem.

Taking Travel Photos with the Leica Q3 43

The Leica Q3 43's small size, powerful performance, and excellent image quality make it a great option for travel photography. From busy city streets to tranquil countryside, travel photography frequently entails capturing a wide range of scenes, and the Leica Q3 43 is adaptable enough to handle it all. The camera's 60 MP full-frame sensor, sharp 43mm f/1.7 lens, and user-friendly settings make it ideal for recording your travels. Here's how to get the most out of your Leica Q3 43 for taking pictures when traveling.

Small and Lightweight Design

The Leica Q3 43's portability is one of its key benefits for trip photography. It's a reasonably small and light camera that won't burden you on lengthy trips or city tours, weighing just over 700 grams (with the battery and memory card). Additionally, the design makes sure that it doesn't attract too much notice, which is particularly helpful for candid street photography or in busy tourist areas.

Reasons it's excellent for travel

- **Portability:** You won't have to worry about lugging about a heavy camera because of its small size, which makes it simple to load into a backpack.
- **Discreet Shooting:** The Q3's simple design makes it easy to be discrete and record unscripted, natural moments, whether you're shooting in crowded marketplaces or peaceful villages.

Adaptability to Various Travel Photography Styles

There are many different types of travel photography, ranging from street photography and portraiture to landscape and architectural photography.

The Leica Q3 43's robust sensor and adaptable 43mm lens allow it to shine in each of these categories.

- **Street Photography:** The natural perspective that a 43mm lens provides makes it ideal for street photography. It provides a sufficiently broad focal length to record unguarded moments of people going about their everyday lives while preserving an air of intimacy and genuineness. Additionally, you can isolate subjects with a shallow depth of field with the f/1.7 aperture, which is useful for portraiture or for highlighting details in a busy street scene.

- **Landscape Photography:** The 43mm lens can still produce excellent landscape images even if it is not a wide-angle lens. This is particularly true when you wish to highlight certain aspects in a picture, such as a winding road, a far-off mountain peak, or a complex architectural element. You can capture a great deal of information in your landscape photos with the Q3's high-resolution 60 MP sensor, which is especially helpful for large prints or cropping photos in post-processing without sacrificing clarity.

- **Portraits:** When you want to focus on your subject and create a creamy, blurred background, the f/1.7 lens and big full-frame sensor are ideal. The short depth of field produces that lovely bokeh effect that helps the subject stand out, whether you're taking pictures in a more controlled environment or people you encounter while traveling.

- **Architecture and aspects:** Visiting famous structures, monuments, and fine aspects of the local way of life are common travel destinations. The Q3's 60 MP resolution is excellent for capturing architectural details, such as delicate building lines or textured stonework. The focal length of the lens also aids in taking closer, more detailed pictures of architectural details as well as wide-angle pictures of large structures.

Personalization and Manual Controls

- The tactile manual controls on the Leica Q3 43 are well known for allowing you complete creative control over your images. You can easily make changes while on the fly without navigating menus thanks to the tactile dials for shutter speed, aperture, and ISO. When shooting in dynamic travel scenarios, where light conditions might vary quickly, this is extremely helpful.

- **Customizable Settings:** To improve productivity and enable fast access to the settings you use most often, you can create unique buttons and features. For instance, you can choose a custom button to represent the several focusing modes you frequently move between. When using manual focus mode, the focus peaking option can also be quite useful, particularly in low light or when you want to guarantee accurate focus.

Superb Image Quality

- The Leica Q3 43's 60 MP full-frame sensor produces remarkably crisp, deep-field, and high-quality images. When photographing in a variety of settings, such as bright, sunny vistas or softly lit streets, this is a big advantage. High contrast scenarios are handled by the camera flawlessly, guaranteeing that details of the highlights and shadows are caught.

- **Low-Light Performance:** Traveling frequently puts you in low-light conditions, such as photographing a sunset or in poorly lit interiors. The Q3 43's large aperture and high sensitivity sensor allow it to function well in low light. When working in less-than-ideal lighting circumstances, you have more versatility because you can shoot at high ISO levels without creating excessive noise.
- **Dynamic Range:** The Q3's dynamic range guarantees that you can preserve clarity in both the image's brightest and darkest regions. You'll have a wide range of tones in your shot, whether you're photographing the bright sun over a beach or the deep shadows of an alley.

Quick Autofocus and Precise Monitoring

Capturing fast-moving subjects, such as people in crowded marketplaces, wildlife, or moving cars, is one of the difficulties of travel photography. With Eye-Tracking AF and continuous focusing modes, the Leica Q3 43 boasts quick and precise autofocus. This ensures that you don't miss any crucial moments by making it simple to rapidly lock focus on things.

How it facilitates travel photography

- **Quick Action Shots:** The Q3 43's autofocus mechanism will guarantee that your subjects are focused and sharp whether you're photographing local sports or a bustling market.
- **Eye Detection:** This feature makes sure that your subject's eyes are always the main focus of your picture, whether you're taking street or portrait photos.

Sturdiness and Weatherproofing

Rain, dust, and extremely high or low temperatures are all inevitable challenges for your equipment when traveling. With weather sealing that shields it from dust and water splashes, the Leica Q3 43 is designed to withstand it. It is appropriate for the majority of travel situations even though it is not completely waterproof because it can withstand mild rain and dusty conditions.

Calmness of Mind

- **Built-in Durability:** You may travel in uncertain conditions with peace of mind knowing that the Q3 is weather sealed, allowing you to concentrate on your images without worrying too much about the weather.

Portability and Battery Life

Battery life is a common issue with travel photography, particularly when you're out for extended shooting sessions. Although the Leica Q3 43 has an excellent battery life, it's always a good idea to have extra batteries on hand, especially for extended trips or when shooting in far-flung places.

Solutions for Portable Charging

- **Portable Chargers:** Bring a portable power bank if you want to be out shooting for a long time. You may always be prepared for the next shot by using the appropriate adapter to recharge your Q3 while you're on the run.

Features That Make Travel Easy

There are numerous travel-friendly features available with the Leica Q3 43.
- **Full HD Video:** The Q3's 4K video capability enables you to record both still images and excellent travel films.
- **Touchscreen and Live View:** You may take pictures from low perspectives or in crowded settings with greater freedom thanks to the tilting touchscreen.
- **Quick Startup Time:** You won't miss any impromptu moments while traveling because the camera is prepared to shoot in a matter of seconds.

Final Thoughts

In conclusion, the Leica Q3 43 is an amazing camera that blends strong functions with beautiful design. It's simple to use and produces excellent results whether you're a professional or just a hobbyist photographer. With its striking details and vibrant colors, the image quality is excellent for both portraits and landscapes. The 28mm lens of the camera provides a broad perspective while yet focusing on minute details. Don't be fooled by its small size and light weight; it has a powerful performance. The controls are straightforward enough that you can concentrate on your imagination rather than fiddling with intricate settings and the focusing performs admirably. The Leica Q3 43 is unique because it combines cutting-edge technology with the classic excellence for which Leica is renowned. It's about assisting you in capturing the world in a way that seems intuitive and natural, not just about snapping photos. It will provide you with the desired outcomes with little effort, regardless of whether you're shooting in brilliant daylight or low light. Overall, the Leica Q3 43 is a fantastic choice if you're searching for a camera that's simple to operate, produces stunning images, and fits comfortably in your palm. It seems like an extension of your artistic vision, is long-lasting, and produces amazing images.

INDEX

Q

R

www.ingramcontent.com/pod-product-compliance
Lightning Source LLC
LaVergne TN
LVHW081758050326
832903LV00027B/2001